CHINA'S CURRENCY AND ECONOMIC ISSUES

CHINA'S CURRENCY AND ECONOMIC ISSUES

W. M. MORRISON
M. LABONTE
AND
J. E. SANFORD

Novinka Books
An imprint of Nova Science Publishers, Inc.
New York

NOTICE TO THE READER

Library of Congress Cataloging-in-Publication Data:
China's currency and economic issues / Wayne M. Morrison, Marc Labonte, and Jonathan E. Sanford.
    p. cm.
Includes index.
ISBN 1-59454-934-6
1. Monetary policy--China. 2. Currency question--China. 3. Foreign exchange rates--China. 4. China--Economic policy--2000- 5. United States--Commercial policy. 6. China--Foreign economic relations--United States. 7. United States--Foreign economic relations--China. I. Labonte, Marc. II. Morrison, Wayne M. China's currency peg. III. Morrison, Wayne M. China's exchange rate peg. IV. Sanford, Jonathan E. China's currency.
 HG1285.C48263   2004
332.4'5640951--dc22   2005037216

Published by Nova Science Publishers, Inc. ✦ *New York*

CONTENTS

PREFACE

China has a policy of pegging its currency (the yuan) to the U.S. dollar. If the yuan is undervalued against the dollar, there are likely to be both benefits and costs to the U.S. economy. It would mean that imported Chinese goods are cheaper than they would be if the yuan were market determined. This lowers prices for U.S. consumers and diminishes inflationary pressures. It also lowers prices for U.S. firms that use imported inputs (such as parts) in their production, making such firms more competitive. Critics of China's peg point to the large and growing U.S. trade deficit with China as evidence that the yuan is undervalued and harmful to the U.S. economy. The relationship is more complex, for a number of reasons. First, while China runs a large trade surplus with the United States, it runs a significant trade deficit with the rest of the world. Second, an increasing level of Chinese exports are from foreign invested companies in China that have shifted production there to take advantage of China's abundant low cost labor. Third, the deficit masks the fact that China has become one of the fastest growing markets for U.S. exports. Finally, the trade deficit with China accounted for 23% of the sum of total U.S. bilateral trade deficits in 2004, indicating that the overall trade deficit is not caused by the exchange rate policy of one country, but rather the shortfall between U.S. saving and investment. This new book presents a coherent examination of the details behind China's currency policies as they relate to outside factors.

Chapter 1

CHINA'S CURRENCY PEG: A SUMMARY OF THE ECONOMIC ISSUES[*]

Wayne M. Morrison and Marc Labonte

SUMMARY

The continued rise in the U.S.-China trade imbalance has led to complaints from various U.S. manufacturing firms and workers. Some Members of Congress assert that China's policy of pegging its currency (the yuan) to the U.S. dollar constitutes a form of currency manipulation, maintained to make Chinese exports cheaper, and its imports more expensive, and that this policy has negatively affected U.S. employment in several sectors. This report evaluates that assertion, and considers other effects China's peg has on the U.S. economy. These include the beneficial effects on consumption, interest rates, and investment spending. Nationwide, these effects should offset job loss in the trade sector, at least in the medium term. Several bills have been introduced in the 109th Congress to address China's currency policy, including H.R. 1216, H.R. 1498, H.R. 1575, S. 14, S. 295, S. 377, and S. 593; some would impose trade sanctions against China unless it accepted a market-based system of currency valuation. This report summarizes CRS Report RL32165, *China's Exchange Rate Peg:*

---

[*] Excerpted from CRS Report RS21625, dated April 25, 2005.

Economic Issues and Options for U.S. Trade Policy, and will be updated as events warrant.

China pegs its currency, the yuan (also called the renminbi), to the U.S. dollar. Under this system, China's central bank issues a reference dollar/yuan exchange rate along with a limited band (about 0.3%) in which the reference rate is allowed to fluctuate. This system has been in place with a peg of about 8.3 yuan to the dollar since 1994.[1] The Chinese central bank maintains this peg by buying (or selling) as many dollar-denominated assets in exchange for newly printed yuan as needed to eliminate excess demand (supply) for the yuan. As a result, the exchange rate between the yuan and the dollar basically stays the same, despite changing economic factors which could otherwise cause the yuan to either appreciate or depreciate relative to the dollar. Under a floating exchange rate system, the relative demand for the two countries' goods and assets would determine the exchange rate of the yuan to the dollar. Many economists contend that for the first several years of the peg, the fixed value was likely close to the market value. But in the past few years, economic conditions have changed such that the yuan would likely have appreciated if it had been floating.[2] Because its currency is not fully convertible in international markets, and because it maintains tight restrictions and controls over capital transactions, China can maintain the exchange rate peg and still use monetary policy to pursue domestic goals (such as full employment).[3]

U.S. CONCERNS ABOUT CHINA'S CURRENCY PEG

Many U.S. policymakers and business and labor representatives have charged that China's currency is significantly undervalued vis-à-vis the U.S. dollar (by as much as 40%), making Chinese exports to the United States cheaper, and U.S. exports to China more expensive, than they would be if exchange rates were determined by market forces. They further argue that the undervalued currency has contributed to the burgeoning U.S. trade deficit with China (which has risen from $30 billion in 1994 to $162 billion in 2004) and has hurt U.S. production and employment in several U.S. manufacturing sectors (such as textiles and apparel and furniture) that are forced to compete domestically and internationally against "artificially" low-cost goods from China. Furthermore, some analysts contend that China's currency peg induces other East Asian countries to intervene in currency markets in order to keep their currencies weak against the dollar in order to compete with Chinese goods.[4] Several groups are pressing the Bush Administration to pressure China to either revalue its currency (by increasing the band in which it is allowed to be traded in China) or to allow it to float freely in international markets. President Bush on a number of occasions has criticized China's currency peg, stating that exchange rates should be determined by market forces.

CHINA'S CONCERNS ABOUT ITS CURRENCY PEG

Chinese officials argue that its currency peg policy is not meant to favor exports over imports, but instead to foster economic stability by tying its currency to the U.S. dollar at a constant level, as many other countries do. They have expressed concern that abandoning the peg could spark an economic crisis in China and would especially be damaging to its export industries at a time when painful economic reforms (such as closing down inefficient state-owned enterprises) are being implemented. They further contend that the Chinese banking system is too underdeveloped and burdened with heavy debt to be able to deal effectively with possible speculative pressures that could occur with a fully convertible currency. The combination of a convertible currency and poorly regulated financial system is seen to be one of the causes of the 1997-1998 Asian financial crisis. Chinese officials view economic stability as critical to sustaining political stability; they fear an appreciated currency could cause deflation, reduce employment, and lower wages in several sectors, and thus could cause worker unrest. Chinese officials claim that during the Asian crisis, when several other nations sharply devalued their currencies, China "held the line" by not devaluing its currency (which might have prompted a new round of destructive devaluations across Asia). This policy was highly praised by U.S. officials, including President Clinton. During a visit to China in September 2003 by U.S. Treasury Secretary John Snow, Chinese officials stated that, while making the yuan fully convertible was a long term goal, China had no immediate plans to eliminate the peg. However, Chinese officials have pledged implement certain financial reforms, and in October 2003, they agreed to a U.S. proposal to set up a joint technical cooperation program to promote the development of China's financial markets and to examine ways China can move more quickly towards a floating exchange rate.

ECONOMIC CONSEQUENCES OF CHINA'S CURRENCY PEG

If the yuan is undervalued against the dollar, as many critics charge, then there are benefits and costs of this policy for the economies of both China and the United States.

Implications of the Peg for China's Economy

If the yuan is undervalued, then Chinese exports to the United States are likely cheaper than they would be if the currency were freely traded, providing a boost to China's export industries (which employ millions of workers and are a major source of China's productivity gains). Eliminating exchange rate risk through a peg also increases the attractiveness of China as a destination for foreign investment in export-oriented production facilities. However, an undervalued currency makes imports more expensive, hurting Chinese consumers and Chinese firms that import parts, machinery, and raw materials. Such a policy, in effect, benefits Chinese exporting firms (many of which are owned by foreign multinational corporations) at the expense of non-exporting Chinese firms, especially those that rely on imported goods. This may impede the most efficient allocation of resources in the Chinese economy. The accumulation of large foreign exchange reserves by China may make it easier for Chinese officials to move more quickly toward adopting a fully convertible currency (if the government feels it could defend the currency against speculative pressures). However, the accumulation of large foreign exchange reserves also entails opportunity costs for China: such funds (instead of sitting in the central bank) could be used to fund China's massive development needs, such as infrastructure improvements.

Implications of the Peg for The U.S. Economy

Effect on Exporters and Import-Competitors

When a fixed exchange rate causes the yuan to be less expensive than it would be if it were determined by supply and demand, it causes Chinese exports to be relatively inexpensive and U.S. exports to China to be relatively expensive. As a result, U.S. exports and the production of U.S. goods and services that compete with Chinese imports fall, in the short run.

(Many of the affected firms are in the manufacturing sector.[5]) This causes the trade deficit to rise and reduces aggregate demand in the short run, all else equal. On the other hand, over the long run, the fixed exchange rate encourages trade (and investment) between the two countries by eliminating exchange rate risk. The reduced risk could make both imports and exports higher than under a floating system.[6]

Effect on U.S. Consumers and Certain Producers

A society's economic well-being is usually measured not by how much it can produce, but how much it can consume. An undervalued yuan that lowers the price of imports from China allows the United States to increase its consumption through an improvement in the terms-of-trade. Since changes in aggregate spending are only temporary, from a long-term perspective the lasting effect of an undervalued yuan is to increase the purchasing power of U.S. consumers. Imports from China are not limited to consumption goods. U.S. producers also import capital equipment and inputs to final products from China. An undervalued yuan lowers the price of these U.S. products, increasing their output.

Effect on U.S. Borrowers

An undervalued yuan also has an effect on U.S. borrowers. When the U.S. runs a current account deficit with China, an equivalent amount of capital flows from China to the United States, as can be seen in the U.S. balance of payments accounts. This occurs because the Chinese central bank or private Chinese citizens are investing in U.S. assets, which allows more U.S. capital investment in plant and equipment to take place than would otherwise occur. Capital investment increases because the greater demand for U.S. assets puts downward pressure on U.S. interest rates, and firms are now willing to make investments that were previously unprofitable. This increases aggregate spending in the short run, all else equal, and also increases the size of the economy in the long run by increasing the capital stock.

Private firms are not the only beneficiaries of the lower interest rates caused by the capital inflow (trade deficit) from China. Interest-sensitive household spending, on goods such as consumer durables and housing, is also higher than it would be if capital from China did not flow into the United States. In addition, a large proportion of the U.S. assets bought by the Chinese, particularly by the central bank, are U.S. Treasury securities, which fund U.S. federal budget deficits. According to the U.S. Treasury Department, China (as of February 2005) held $196.5 billion in U.S.

Treasury securities, making China the second largest foreign holder of such securities, after Japan. If the U.S. trade deficit with China were eliminated, Chinese capital would no longer flow into this country on net, and the government would have to find other buyers of its U.S. Treasuries. This would increase the government's interest payments.

Net Effect on the U.S. Economy

In the medium run, an undervalued yuan neither increases nor decreases aggregate demand in the United States. Rather, it leads to a compositional shift in U.S. production, away from U.S. exporters and import-competing firms toward the firms that benefit from Chinese capital flows. Thus, it is expected to have no medium or long run effect on aggregate U.S. employment or unemployment. As evidence, one can consider that the U.S. had a historically large and growing trade deficit throughout the 1990s at a time when unemployment reached a three-decade low. However, the gains and losses in employment and production caused by the trade deficit will not be dispersed evenly across regions and sectors of the economy: on balance, some areas will gain while others will lose. And by shifting the composition of U.S. output to a higher capital base, the size of the economy would be larger in the long run as a result of the capital inflow/trade deficit.

Although the compositional shift in output has no negative effect on aggregate U.S. output and employment in the long run, there may be adverse short-run consequences. If output in the trade sector falls more quickly than the output of U.S. recipients of Chinese capital rises, aggregate spending and employment could temporarily fall. This is more likely to be a concern if the economy is already sluggish than if it is at full employment. Otherwise, it is likely that government macroeconomic policy adjustment and market forces can quickly compensate for any decline of output in the trade sector by expanding other elements of aggregate demand.

The U.S.-China Trade Deficit in the Context of the Overall U.S. Trade Deficit

While China is a large trading partner, it accounted for only 13.4% of U.S. imports in 2004 and 23% of the sum of the bilateral trade deficits. Over a span of several years, a country with a floating exchange rate can run an ongoing overall trade deficit for only one reason: a domestic imbalance between saving and investment. This has been the case for the United States over the past two decades, where saving as a share of gross domestic product (GDP) has been in gradual decline. On the one hand, the U.S. has high rates of productivity growth and strong economic fundamentals that are conducive to high rates of capital investment. On the other hand, it has a chronically low household saving rate, and recently a negative government saving rate as a result of the budget deficit. As long as Americans save little, foreigners will use their saving to finance profitable investment opportunities in the U.S.; the trade deficit is the result. [7] The returns to foreign-owned capital will flow to foreigners instead of Americans, but the returns to U.S. labor utilizing foreign-owned capital will flow to U.S. labor.

According to Chinese statistics, more than half of what China exports to the world is produced by foreign-invested firms in China, including U.S. companies, which, in many cases, have shifted production to China in order to gain access to China's low-cost labor. (The returns to capital of U.S. owned firms in China flow to Americans.) Such firms import raw materials and components (much of which come from East Asia) for assembly in China. As a result, China tends to run trade deficits with East Asian countries and trade surpluses with countries with high consumer demand, such as the United States. Overall, in 2004, China had a $32 billion trade surplus (Chinese data), indicating that China had a $130 billion trade deficit with the world excluding the United States. These factors imply that much of the increase in U.S. imports (and hence, the rising U.S. trade deficit with China) is largely the result of China becoming a production platform for many foreign companies, rather than unfair Chinese trade policies.

For these reasons, economists generally are more concerned with the overall trade deficit than bilateral trade balances. Because of comparative advantage, it is natural that a country will have some trading partners from which it imports more, and some trading partners to which it exports more. For example, the U.S. has a trade deficit with Austria and a trade surplus with the Netherlands even though both countries use the euro, which floats against with the dollar. Of concern to the United States is that its low saving rate makes it so reliant on foreigners to finance its investment opportunities, and not the fact that much of the capital comes from China. If the U.S. did not borrow from China as a result of the exchange rate peg, it would still have to borrow from other countries.

Proposed Legislation in the 109th Congress

Eleven bills were introduced in the 108th that sought to address China's currency policy or countries that "manipulated" their exchange rates. In the 109th Congress, S.14 (Stabenow) S. 295 (Schumer), and H.R. 1575 (Spratt) would raise U.S. tariffs on Chinese goods by an additional 27.5% unless

China appreciated its currency to a level at or near market value. S. 377 (Lieberman) directs the President to negotiate with countries that manipulate their currency and to institute proceedings under the relevant U.S. and international trade laws if an agreement is not reached. In addition, H.R. 1216 (English) and S. 593 (Collins) would apply U.S. countervailing laws (dealing with government subsidies) to nonmarket economies, such as China. Many Members contend that China's currency peg constitutes a form of government subsidy. H.R. 1498 (Tim Ryan) would apply U.S. countervailing laws against any nation that manipulated its currency.

On April 6, 2005, the Senate failed (by a vote of 33 to 67) to table an amendment, S.Amdt. 309 (Schumer) to S. 600 (Foreign Affairs Authorization Act), which would impose a 27.5% tariff on Chinese goods if China failed to substantially appreciate its currency to market levels. In response to the vote, the Senate leadership moved to allow a vote on S. 295 (which has same language as S.Amdt. 309) no later than July 27, 2005.

ENDNOTES

[1] Prior to this time, China maintained a dual exchange rate system: an official exchange rate of about 5.8 yuan to the dollar and a market swap rate (used mainly for trade transactions) of about 8.7 yuan to the dollar (at the end of 1993). The reforms in 1994 unified the two rates.

[2] Many analysts argue that the sharp increase in China's foreign exchange reserves (which grew from $168 billion in 2000 to $403 billion in 2003, to $610 billion at the end of 2004) is one indicator that the yuan is undervalued.

[3] The currency is convertible on a current account basis (such as for trade transactions), but not on a capital account basis (for various types of financial flows, such as portfolio investment). In addition, holdings of foreign exchange by Chinese firms and individuals are closely regulated by the government.

[4] See Prepared Remarks of Dr. C. Fred Bergsten, President, Institute for International Economics, before the House Small Business Committee, June 25, 2003.

[5] There is a long run trend that is moving U.S. production away from manufacturing and toward the service sector. U.S. employment in manufacturing as a share of total nonagricultural employment has fallen from 31.8% in 1960 to 22.4% in 1980 to 12.8% in 2002. This trend is much larger than the Chinese currency issue, and is caused by

changing technology (which requires fewer workers to produce the same number of goods) and comparative advantage. With enhanced globalization, the theory of comparative advantage predicts the U.S. will produce knowledge- and technology-intensive goods that it is best at producing for trade with countries, such as China, who are better at producing labor-intensive goods. Since many manufactured goods are labor-intensive, comparative advantage leads to more manufacturing abroad, and less in the United States. Over time, it is likely that the trend shifting manufacturing abroad will continue regardless of China's currency peg.

[6] Putting exchange rate issues aside, most economists maintain that trade is a win-win situation for the economy as a whole, but produces losers within the economy. This view derives from the principle of comparative advantage, which states that trade shifts production to the goods a country is relatively talented at producing from goods it is relatively untalented at producing. As trade expands, production of goods with a comparative disadvantage will decline in the U.S., to the detriment of workers and investors in those sectors (offset by higher employment and profits in sectors with a comparative advantage). Economists generally argue that free trade should be pursued because the gains from trade are large enough that the losers from trade can be compensated by the winners, and the winners will still be better off. See CRS Report RL32059.

[7] Nations, such as the United States, that fail to save enough to meet their investment needs must obtain savings from other countries with high savings rates. By obtaining foreign investment (in effect, borrowing), the United States can consume more (including more imports) than it would if investment were funded by domestic savings alone — this results in a trade deficit.

Chapter 2

CHINA'S EXCHANGE RATE PEG: ECONOMIC ISSUES AND OPTIONS FOR U.S. TRADE POLICY[*]

Wayne Morrison and Marc Labonte

SUMMARY

The continued rise in the U.S.-China trade imbalance and complaints from U.S. manufacturing firms and workers over the competitive challenges posed by cheap Chinese imports have led several Members to call for a more aggressive U.S. stance against certain Chinese trade policies they deem to be unfair, such as China's policy of pegging its currency (the yuan) to the U.S. dollar. Some Members assert this policy constitutes a form of "currency manipulation" intended to give China an unfair trade advantage and is contributing to the loss of U.S. manufacturing jobs.

If the yuan is undervalued against the dollar, there are likely to be both benefits and costs to the U.S. economy. It would mean that imported Chinese goods are cheaper than they would be if the yuan were market determined. This lowers prices for U.S. consumers and diminishes inflationary pressures. It also lowers prices for U.S. firms that use

---

[*] Excerpted from CRS Report RL32165, dated May 10, 2005.

imported inputs (such as parts) in their production, making such firms more competitive. When the U.S. runs a trade deficit with the Chinese, this requires a capital inflow from China to the United States. This, in turn, lowers U.S. interest rates and increases U.S. investment spending. On the negative side, lower priced goods from China may hurt U.S. industries that compete with those products, diminishing their production and employment. In addition, an undervalued yuan makes U.S. exports to China more expensive, thus diminishing the level of U.S. exports to China and job opportunities for U.S. workers in those sectors. However, in the long run, trade can affect only the composition of employment, not its overall level. Thus, inducing China to appreciate its currency would likely benefit some U.S. economic sectors, but would harm others, including U.S. consumers.

Critics of China's peg point to the large and growing U.S. trade deficit with China as evidence that the yuan is undervalued and harmful to the U.S. economy. The relationship is more complex, for a number of reasons. First, while China runs a large trade surplus with the United States, it runs a significant trade deficit with the rest of the world. Second, an increasing level of Chinese exports are from foreign-invested companies in China that have shifted production there to take advantage of China's abundant low cost labor. Third, the deficit masks the fact that China has become one of the fastest growing markets for U.S. exports. Finally, the trade deficit with China accounted for 23% of the sum of total U.S. bilateral trade deficits in 2004, indicating that the overall trade deficit is not caused by the exchange rate policy of one country, but rather the shortfall between U.S. saving and investment.
Several bills have been introduced in the 109th Congress to address China's currency policy, including H.R. 1216, H.R. 1498, H.R. 1575, S. 14, S. 295, S. 377, and S. 593; some would impose trade sanctions against China unless it accepted a market-based currency system. While the Bush Administration has pressed China to make the yuan fully convertible, it has sought to avoid confrontation with China on the issue. Instead, it has offered technical assistance to China to help it make the type of reforms to its financial system that, if implemented, will induce China to move more quickly toward adopting a more flexible currency regime. This report will be updated as events warrant.

China pegs its currency, the yuan (or renminbi), to the U.S. dollar.[1] Under this system, China's central bank issues a reference dollar/yuan exchange rate along with a limited band (about 0.3%) in which the reference rate is allowed to fluctuate. This system has been in place with a peg of about 8.3 yuan to the dollar since 1994. Many economists contend that for the first several years of the peg, the fixed value was likely close to the market value. But in the past few years, economic conditions have changed such that the yuan would likely have appreciated if it had been floating. This situation has raised concerns in the United States, but the Chinese, with concerns about their own economy, have been reluctant to alter the peg.

U.S. CONCERNS ABOUT CHINA'S CURRENCY PEG

Many U.S. policymakers and business and labor representatives have charged that China's currency is significantly undervalued vis-a-vis the U.S. dollar by as much as 40%, making Chinese exports to the United States cheaper, and U.S. exports to China more expensive, than they would be if exchange rates were determined by market forces. They further argue that the undervalued currency has contributed to the burgeoning U.S. trade deficit with China (which has risen from $30 billion in 1994 to $162 billion in 2004) and has hurt U.S. production and employment in several U.S. manufacturing sectors (such as textiles and apparel and furniture) that are forced to compete domestically and internationally against "artificially" low-cost goods from China.

Furthermore, some analysts contend that China's currency peg induces other East Asian countries to intervene in currency markets in order to keep their currencies weak against the dollar to remain competitive with Chinese goods.[2] Several groups are pressing the Bush Administration to pressure China either to revalue its currency (by increasing the band in which it is allowed to be traded in China) or to allow it to float freely in international markets. During an interview with CNBC's Ron Insana on September 5, 2003, President Bush criticized China's currency peg and stated that exchange rates should be determined by market forces.

CHINA'S CONCERNS ABOUT ABANDONING ITS CURRENCY PEG

Chinese officials argue that its currency peg policy is not meant to favor exports over imports, but instead to foster economic stability by tying its currency to the U.S. dollar at a constant level, as many other countries do. They have expressed concern that abandoning the peg could spark an economic crisis in China and would especially be damaging to its export industries at a time when painful economic reforms (such as closing down inefficient state-owned enterprises) are being implemented. They further contend that the Chinese banking system is too underdeveloped and burdened with heavy debt to be able to deal effectively with possible speculative pressures that could occur with a fully convertible currency. The combination of a convertible currency and poorly regulated financial system is seen to be one of the causes of the 1997-1998 Asian financial crisis.

Chinese officials view economic stability as critical to sustaining political stability; they fear an appreciating currency could reduce foreign investment, cause deflation, reduce employment, and lower wages in several sectors, and thus could cause worker unrest. Chinese officials also point out that during the Asian crisis, when several other nations sharply devalued their currencies, China "held the line" by not devaluing its currency (which might have prompted a new round of destructive devaluations across Asia). This policy was highly praised by U.S. officials, including President Clinton. During a visit to China in September 2003 by U.S. Treasury Secretary John Snow, Chinese officials stated that, while making the exchange rate regime more flexible was a long-term goal, China had no immediate plans to eliminate the peg, but was considering certain financial reforms. In October 2003, Chinese officials agreed to a U.S. proposal to set up a joint technical cooperation program with the United States to facilitate cooperation and communication between financial experts in both countries to promote the development of China's financial markets and to examine ways China can move more quickly towards a floating exchange rate.[3]

THE ECONOMICS OF FIXED EXCHANGE RATES

How the Peg Operates

China maintains a fixed exchange rate with the United States, where the Chinese central bank buys or sells as much currency as is needed to keep the yuan-dollar exchange rate constant at 8.3 yuan per dollar.[4] The primary alternative to this arrangement would be a floating exchange rate, as the U.S. maintains with the Euro area, in which supply and demand in the marketplace causes the euro-dollar exchange rate to continually fluctuate. Under a floating exchange rate system, the relative demand for the two countries' goods and assets would determine the exchange rate of the yuan to the dollar. If the demand for Chinese goods or assets increased, more yuan would be demanded to purchase those goods and assets, and the yuan would rise in value (if the central bank kept the supply of yuan constant) to restore equilibrium.

When a fixed exchange rate is equal in value to the rate that would prevail in the market if it were floating, the central bank does not need to take any action to maintain the peg. However, over time economic circumstances change, and with them change the relative demand for a country's currency. If the Chinese had maintained a floating exchange rate, appreciation would likely have occurred in the past few years for a number of reasons. For instance, productivity and quality improvements in China may have increased the relative demand for Chinese goods and foreign direct investment in China. For the exchange rate peg to be maintained when economic circumstances have changed requires the central bank to supply or remove as much currency as is needed to bring supply back in line with market demand, which it does by increasing or decreasing foreign exchange reserves. This is shown in the following accounting identity, used to record the international balance of payments:

Net Current Account = Net Capital Account
[(Exports-Imports) + Net Unilateral = [(Private Capital Outflow-Inflow)
+ Transfers] Change in Foreign Exchange Reserves]

Thus, anytime net exports (exports less imports) or net private capital inflows (private capital inflows less outflows) increase, foreign exchange reserves must increase by an equivalent amount to maintain the exchange rate peg. This is the current situation for the Chinese central bank. At the prevailing exchange rate peg, there is excess demand for yuan (equivalently, excess supply of dollars). For the central bank to maintain the peg, it must increase its foreign reserves by buying dollars from the public in exchange for newly printed yuan. As seen in Table 1, foreign reserves grew from $22 billion in 1993, to $168 billion in 2000, to $610 billion at year-end 2004. About half of these reserves, at a minimum, are non-U.S. assets.[5] China's foreign exchange holdings rose by 39% in 2003 (over the previous year) and by 51.2% in 2004. As long as the Chinese are willing to accumulate dollar reserves, they can continue to maintain the peg.[6] Rather than hold U.S. dollars, which earn no interest, the Chinese central bank mostly holds U.S. financial securities — primarily U.S. Treasury securities, but also likely U.S. Agency securities (e.g., the obligations of Fannie Mae and Freddie Mac).

Table 1. China's Foreign Exchange Reserves and Overall Current Account Surplus: 1990-2004

Year	Cumulative Foreign Exchange Reserves			Current Account Balance
	billions of $	% of GDP	% of imports	billions of $
1990	29.6	7.6	54.9	11.9
1991	43.7	10.8	68.4	13.1
1992	20.6	4.3	25.2	6.2
1993	22.4	3.7	21.6	-11.7
1994	52.9	9.8	45.8	6.5
1995	75.4	10.8	57.1	1.3
1996	107.0	13.1	77.1	5.6
1997	142.8	15.9	100.4	32.5
1998	149.2	15.8	106.4	31.2
1999	157.7	15.9	95.1	21.1
2000	168.3	15.6	74.8	20.5
2001	215.6	18.1	88.5	17.5
2002	291.1	23.5	98.6	35.4
2003	403.3	28.1	97.7	31.4
2004	609.9	38.5	108.6	58.7

Source:Economist Intelligence Unit and International Monetary Fund.
Note: Data for 2004 are estimates.

But maintaining a peg is not the only reason the Chinese government could be accumulating foreign exchange reserves. Foreign exchange reserves are necessary to finance international trade (in the presence of capital controls) and to fend off speculation against one's currency. One would expect a country to increase its foreign reserves for these purposes as its economy and trade grew. However, Table 1 illustrates that the increase in foreign exchange reserves in China has significantly outpaced the growth of GDP or imports in the last couple of years.

Economic activity, including the level of imports and exports, is not determined by the nominal exchange rate, but by the real (inflation-adjusted) exchange rate. Because the United States and China have had roughly similar increases in the overall price levels in the past 10 years (29% in China vs. 24% in the United States), the difference between the real and nominal rate has been small between 1994 and 2003. However, China had much higher inflation than the United States from 1994-1997, so the real and nominal exchange rates diverged considerably during that time. The real exchange rate appreciated from China's perspective, making their exports more expensive and U.S. imports cheaper. Since then, the real and nominal exchange rates have converged because China's inflation rate has been lower than U.S. inflation in the past few years. This can be seen in Figure 1. In 2003, the Chinese exchange rate reached its lowest level since 1994 in real terms, from the Chinese perspective, making their exports progressively less expensive since 1997.[7] However, inflation was higher in China than the U.S. in 2004, so their real exchange rate slightly appreciated from its 2003 value.

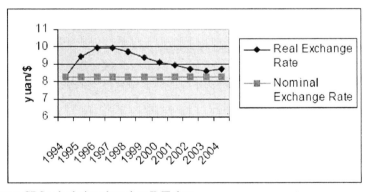

Source: CRS calculations based on IMF data.
Note: Real exchange adjusted for inflation using the consumer price index, based on 2000 prices.

Figure 1. Real and Nominal China-U.S. Exchange Rate

In the long run, real (inflation-adjusted) exchange rates return to their market value whether they are (nominally) fixed or floating. Imagine that the demand for Chinese goods and services were to increase. If the yuan were floating, it would appreciate, as more yuan were acquired to purchase

Chinese goods. It would continue to appreciate until the excess demand for Chinese goods was exhausted (since they are now more expensive in terms of foreign currency), at which point the trade balance would return to its equilibrium level. With a fixed exchange rate, the real exchange rate returns to its market value through price adjustment instead, which takes time. If the exchange rate were fixed below the level that would prevail in the market, Chinese exports would be relatively inexpensive and U.S. imports would be relatively expensive. As long as this situation prevailed, the trade surplus with the United States would persist. The trade surplus (plus net remittances) is equal to the capital flowing from China to the United States. Part of this capital consists of the purchase of U.S. assets by private Chinese citizens. The other portion consists of the accumulation of dollar reserves by the Chinese central bank. By increasing its dollar reserves, the central bank is also increasing the supply of yuan. This causes the inflation rate in China to rise, all else equal.[8] Over time, as prices rise, exports will become more costly abroad and imports less costly. At that point, the trade surplus will return to its equilibrium value. Although the nominal exchange rate never changed, because of the rise in prices, the real exchange rate would now equal the market rate that would prevail if the exchange rate had been floating. Thus, undervaluing a fixed exchange rate does not confer any permanent competitive advantage for a country's exporters and import-competing industries. However, because price adjustment takes time, floating exchange rates return to the real market value much more quickly than fixed exchange rates.

Pros and Cons of a Peg

Fixed exchange rates have a long history of use, including the Bretton Woods system linking the major currencies of the world from the 1940s to the 1960s and the international gold standard before then. There is little consensus among economists and policymakers whether floating or fixed exchange rates are preferable. Both systems, and the many hybrid systems in between, have their advantages and disadvantages. Furthermore, since countries differ so significantly in their economic and demographic conditions, an exchange rate regime that suits one country may be unsuitable for another. Economists identify two main advantages, one economic and one political, to a fixed exchange rate.[9]

Economically, a fixed exchange rate provides *stability* between the country and the partner to which it is linked. This reduces risk and uncertainty in the price of goods, services, and capital between the two countries, thereby fostering greater trade and capital integration between the two. China's focus on attracting foreign direct investment makes stability particularly appealing. The drawback to greater stability is less policy *flexibility* for the country maintaining the peg, in this case China, to use monetary and fiscal policy to offset changes in the business cycle (the U.S. loses no policy flexibility from China's peg). For example, a peg would prevent a country from lowering its interest rates to offset an economic downturn. If it did, capital would flow out of the country to assets with higher interest rates in the rest of the world, and the country would find its currency peg under pressure (since investors would sell the country's currency and buy foreign currency to transfer their capital abroad) until it raised its interest rates.

This loss of flexibility is relatively unimportant for small countries that fix their exchange rate to large neighbors that share the same business cycle, since the large neighbor would also likely be affected by the downturn and lower its interest rates. But the loss in flexibility is costly when a country is tied to a partner to whom it is not closely linked and does not experience similar business cycles, as is arguably the case between the United States and China.

However, China mitigates the loss of flexibility that a country with a fixed exchange rate would normally experience through its use of capital controls (legal barriers restricting access to foreign currency). The currency is convertible on a current account basis (such as for trade transactions), but not on a capital account basis (for various types of financial flows, such as portfolio investment). In addition, nearly all Chinese enterprises are required to turn over their foreign currency holdings to China's state bank in exchange for yuan, and purchases of foreign exchange by individuals and firms in China are closely regulated. Because capital cannot easily leave China when interest rates are lowered, China retains some flexibility over its monetary and fiscal policy despite the fixed exchange rate. Another drawback to fixed exchange rates is the possibility of speculative attacks if investors believe that the central bank is unable to defend the peg. Capital controls also decrease the likelihood of speculative attacks, which have been a major proximate cause of economic crisis in developing countries in recent years, including Southeast Asia, Argentina, and Turkey.[10]

Politically, a fixed exchange rate is seen as a way to enhance the *credibility* of a country's monetary authorities by "tying its hands." Since a fixed exchange rate limits a country's use of discretionary monetary policy, the country is no longer as free to abuse its monetary discretion. Notably, the country is less able to use inflationary monetary policies to stimulate the economy for short-term gain or to finance government spending that has not been financed through tax revenues. Many developing countries with a history of high inflation adopt fixed exchange rates as a way to "break with the past." Once credibility has been established through many years of price stability, the credibility rationale for a fixed exchange rate becomes less important. China's inflation rate never rose higher than 2.8% between 1997 and 2003 (and in some years was negative), and has never exceeded 24.1% (1994) since its transition to a market economy beginning in the late 1970s. Inflation rose to 3.9% in 2004, fueled in part by speculation in real estate, over-investment in certain industries, and rising costs for energy and raw materials. In response, the Chinese Central Bank in October 2004 raised its one year lending rate by a 0.27 percentage point, the first rate hike by the bank in more than nine years.

Fixed exchange rates do not have to be kept constant when economic conditions change; they can be revalued and then fixed at a new rate. Frequent revaluation, however, diminishes the economic benefit of stability and the political benefit of credibility (particularly when the exchange rate is devalued, or revalued downward), which could increase the likelihood of future speculation against the currency.

A CRITIQUE OF VARIOUS ESTIMATES OF THE YUAN'S UNDERVALUATION

Although it is certain that the yuan would appreciate if the central bank were not increasing its foreign reserves, there is no direct way to determine how much it would appreciate. Estimates of the extent of the yuan's undervaluation have been cited in many articles and interviews. This report attempts to evaluate only those estimates in which the author explains how the estimate was derived. It should be noted that many of the estimates were made some time ago, so the yuan may be more or less undervalued at this point than when the estimates were made.

Ernest Preeg, senior fellow at the Manufacturers' Alliance, estimates that the yuan is undervalued by 40%.[11] While this claim is not based on any formal analysis, he uses several rule-of-thumb estimates to reach this conclusion. His first observation is that the increase in Chinese foreign exchange reserves equaled 100% of the Chinese trade surplus less net foreign direct investment (FDI) flows in the first six months of 2002. He concludes that the entire trade surplus less net foreign direct investment would be zero in the absence of the increase in foreign exchange reserves. His second observation is a rule-of-thumb estimate that a 1% decline in the dollar leads to a $10 billion decline in the trade deficit in the United States He then observes that the dollar would need to decline by 40% according to that rule of thumb to eliminate the trade deficit since the U.S. trade deficit equaled about $400 billion in 2002. Since the Chinese trade surplus plus net FDI flows equaled 100% of the increase in foreign exchange reserves, he concludes that if the central bank no longer increased its foreign exchange reserves by letting the yuan float, the surplus less FDI would be zero and the yuan would appreciate by 40%, based on the U.S. ratio.

The Institute for International Economics (IIE) estimates that the yuan is 15-25% undervalued. It argues that the "underlying" current account surplus was 2.5-3% of GDP, larger than the actual surplus (1.5%) (it does not explain why).[12] They then argue that the surplus should be reduced by $50 billion (or 4% of GDP) to return to equilibrium, which would leave China with a deficit of 1-1.5% of GDP in equilibrium. They believe that the revaluation required to achieve this reduction in the current account surplus is unusually large because of the extensive use of imports in the production of Chinese exports. IIE Fellow Morris Goldstein testified that

> These estimates of [yuan] misalignment can be obtained either by solving a trade model for the appreciation of the RMB that would produce equilibrium in China's overall balance of payments, or by gauging the appreciation of the RMB that make a fair contribution to the reduction in global payment imbalances, especially the reduction of the U.S. current-account deficit to a more sustainable level.[13]

Goldman Sachs Economic Research Group has estimated that the yuan is 9.5-15% undervalued.[14] They argue that the current account less FDI should be zero in equilibrium (which means that China would have a current account deficit equal to FDI), which could be accomplished with a 9.5-15% revaluation. This is based on their elasticity estimates that exports would fall 0.2% and imports would rise 0.5% when the exchange rate rose 1%.

All three of these estimates are based on a similar logic, so a few general observations can be made about all of them. A shortcoming of all of the estimates is that they are not the product of theoretically grounded, econometrically estimated economic models. Rather, they are "back of the envelope" estimates based on a few simple "rule of thumb" assumptions. "Rules of thumb" such as the Preeg 10%-$1 billion estimate or the Goldman

Sachs import and export elasticities may not be accurate over time or over large changes in the exchange rate.

The main source of contention in all of the estimates of the yuan's undervaluation is the definition of an "equilibrium" current account balance. All three estimates are defined as the appreciation that would be required for China to attain "equilibrium" in the current account balance. But there is no consensus based on theory or evidence to determine what equilibrium would be; rather, the authors base equilibrium on their own personal opinion.[15] Some economists argue that current account balance would always be close to zero in equilibrium, but this neglects the fact that countries with different saving and investment rates may willingly lend to and borrow from one another for long periods of time.

In fact, all three estimates use an assumption of equilibrium less favorable to China than current account balance. These studies actually call for balance only in official and portfolio borrowing. They still allow for foreign direct investment (FDI) inflows, which means their estimate of China's overall "equilibrium" current account position is actually a deficit. If they had chosen balance (the traditional "equilibrium" measure with a fixed exchange rate) instead of a deficit as their equilibrium benchmark, their estimates of the yuan's undervaluation would have been smaller. Even if portfolio flows are essentially limited by capital controls at present, it is not clear why requiring the Chinese to borrow from the rest of the world is any less unsustainable than the current arrangement where China is lending to the rest of the world. With capital controls and net FDI inflows, increasing foreign reserves is the only way that China can keep its net foreign indebtedness from increasing. And all three measures rule out any accumulation of foreign official reserves for reasons other than to influence the exchange rate.

It is particularly difficult to determine the equilibrium current account balance in China because of the current presence of capital controls. If China were to maintain capital controls after currency reform (if, for example, they revalued the peg rather than let the yuan float), current account balance may be a reasonable assumption. But if capital controls were eliminated, as is typically the case with a floating exchange rate, the economic situation would change entirely —"equilibrium" could now involve persistent borrowing from or lending to the rest of the world by private Chinese citizens, which would result in a corresponding persistent trade deficit or surplus, respectively. If private citizens lent as much to the United States in equilibrium as the Chinese central bank is currently lending (and U.S. lending to China remained unchanged), then the equilibrium market exchange rate would be equal to the current fixed rate, and the trade deficit would remain unchanged. If private capital outflows exceeded the current increase in foreign reserves, the yuan would depreciate. Since China is a country with both a high national saving rate and a high investment rate, it is not clear whether China would be a net borrower (in which case it would run a current account deficit) or lender (current account surplus) if their currency floated and capital controls were abolished. This issue is particularly relevant when the equilibrium exchange rate is defined as "market determined," since capital controls currently prevent portfolio investment flows from being market determined. Bosworth argues that China's high internal saving rate is more than sufficient to finance its investment, so it makes sense for China to offset FDI inflows with official outflows in the form of foreign reserve accumulation rather than run a current account deficit. Therefore, he argues, foreign reserve accumulation should not be considered proof of undervaluation.[16]

IIE and Preeg also base their analysis on their belief that the U.S. trade deficit is unsustainable, and revaluing the yuan would reduce it. If trade and financial markets are rational over the medium run, then the value of the dollar and the size of the trade deficit are never unsustainable — if they were, investors would be unwilling to hold U.S. assets and would sell the dollar, and the trade deficit would decline. There is no widely accepted theoretical approach to determining trade deficit sustainability, and *prima facie* evidence does not suggest the U.S. trade deficit is unsustainable — it has lasted several years, it did not prevent the U.S. economy from achieving record growth and low unemployment in the late 1990s, U.S. investment income paid to foreigners is not large, and there have not been any unusually large or sudden declines in the dollar since the trade deficit emerged.[17]

Furthermore, if the Chinese central bank stopped buying U.S. assets, and hence reduced its bilateral trade deficit with the United States, it is not clear that the overall U.S. trade deficit would fall by a corresponding amount. Other foreigners would still be free to lend to the United States, which could cause its other bilateral trade deficits to widen. Thus, it is not clear that a "fair share" of a reduction in the U.S. trade deficit can be apportioned to the Chinese. On the other hand, if China's overall trade surplus were eliminated, it might still run a bilateral trade surplus with the United States. Even countries with overall trade deficits, including the United States, have some trading partners with whom they run surpluses and some with whom they run deficits.

There are additional criticisms of the Preeg estimate. First, Preeg's conversion of the rule of thumb from dollar terms to percentage of the total trade deficit is without justification. His conversion implies that if the U.S. trade deficit were $1, a 40% decline in the dollar would lower the deficit by $1. By that logic, if the trade deficit were $1 trillion, a 40% decline in the dollar would lower the deficit by $1 trillion. Clearly, a 40% decline in the dollar cannot have such different effects on the trade deficit simply because the dollar value of the trade deficit has changed. Second, Preeg applies his estimate based on U.S. data to the Chinese trade surplus without any supporting evidence. Since the United States and China have different economies, trading patterns, trade balances, and exchange rate regimes, there is no reason to think the estimate would be the same for both countries. He also uses overall and bilateral trade balances interchangeably. There is no reason to think that a 40% decline in the dollar would have the same effect on a $400 billion U.S. overall trade deficit (from which he does not subtract FDI) as a 40% decline in the yuan would have on a $60 billion bilateral Chinese trade surplus less FDI.[18]

There are two other estimates of the yuan's undervaluation based on the theory of purchasing power parity (PPP), the theory that the same good should have the same price in two different countries. If it did not, then arbitrageurs could buy it in the cheaper country and sell it in the more expensive country until the price disparity disappeared. While this simple idea is powerful in theory, it has been proven to be unreliable in reality: prices are consistently lower in developing countries than industrialized countries. Economist Jeffrey Frankel argues that income level can be regressed on the exchange rate using a cross-sample of countries to find a predictable relationship between a country's income level and its equilibrium exchange rate based on PPP. By this measure, he estimates that China's exchange rate was undervalued by 36% in 2000.[19] Newer data is not available, but he speculates that, if anything, the undervaluation has increased since then. He acknowledges a number of caveats to this analysis. First, PPP only holds over the long run, at best, and financial flows can cause even market-determined exchange rates to significantly diverge from PPP for several years. Second, the regression does not control for other factors and only explains 57% of the variation in the data. Third, Frankel argues that any adjustment in the exchange rate should be gradual so as not to be economically disruptive. He also warns that "It is not even true that an appreciation of the renminbi against the dollar would have an immediately noticeable effect on the overall U.S. trade deficit or employment..."[20]

Does international experience suggest what the Chinese current account balance would be in equilibrium? The closest comparison is probably to other East Asian countries, which also grew rapidly and maintained high saving rates in recent decades. The experience of these countries is mixed. From 1980 to 1997, Korea, Malaysia, Philippines, Indonesia, and Thailand typically ran current account deficits, while Hong Kong, Singapore, Taiwan, and Japan (which had already industrialized) typically ran current account surpluses. Since the Asian financial crisis in 1997, all of these countries have run large current account surpluses. This may suggest that the current economic environment is not conducive to developing world borrowing. As seen in Table 2, the same combination of large foreign exchange reserves and a large current account surplus can be seen in several other countries in the region, even though these countries range in their exchange rate regimes from a float (Japan and South Korea) to a currency board (Hong Kong).

Table 2. Foreign Exchange Reserves and Current Account Balance in Selected Asian Countries, 2004 ($ billions and as percent of GDP)

	Foreign Exchange Reserves		Current Account Surplus	
	billions of $	% of GDP	billions of $	% of GDP
Japan	833.9	17.9%	172.1	3.7%
China	609.9	38.6%	58.7	3.7%
Taiwan	241.7	79.2%	18.9	6.2%
South Korea	199.0	30.4%	27.6	4.1%
Hong Kong	123.5	77.4%	13.0	8.1%

Source: Economist Intelligence Unit estimates and official Chinese data.

Another frequently cited estimate of the yuan's undervaluation is based on the *Economist* magazine's Big Mac Index, which estimated that China's currency was undervalued by 58% in December 2004.[21] The *Economist* portrays the Big Mac Index as a "light hearted guide" to exchange rates, and there are important drawbacks to relying too heavily on it. Based on the theory of purchasing power parity, the Big Mac Index compares the price of a McDonald's Big Mac in China to the United States. Since a Big Mac in China was 56% cheaper than in the United States, the index concludes that the yuan is undervalued by that much. But purchasing power parity only applies to tradeable goods, and a Big Mac is not tradeable. In fact, Ong estimates that 94% of the value of a Big Mac comes not from the hamburger itself, but the services associated with the hamburger.[22] These include the wages of employees serving the Big Mac and the rent of the restaurant in which it is eaten, both of which are determined by local factors. Since the hamburger itself is the only tradeable portion of the Big Mac, only a small fraction of the Big Mac's value should be determined by purchasing power parity. As a result, a Big Mac in New York City is more expensive than a Big Mac purchased in the U.S. rural south. Taken literally, the Big Mac Index would imply that a dollar in the rural south is undervalued compared to a dollar in New York City.

TRENDS AND FACTORS IN THE U.S.-CHINA TRADE DEFICIT

Critics of China's currency peg often point to the large and growing U.S.-China trade imbalance as proof that the yuan is significantly undervalued and constitutes an attempt to gain an unfair competitive advantage over the United States in trade. However, bilateral trade balances reflect structural causes as well as exchange rate effects. There are a number of other factors at work that are also important to consider when analyzing the bilateral trade deficit.

First, although China had (according to U.S. statistics) a $162 billion merchandise trade surplus with the United States in 2004, its overall trade surplus was much smaller, only $32 billion (Chinese data), indicating that China had a trade deficit of $130 billion in its trade with the world excluding the United States.[23] In comparison, Japan in 2004 had a $75.2 billion trade surplus with the United States (U.S. data) and $110.5 billion overall trade surplus (Japanese data), indicating that Japan had a trade surplus of $35.3 billion with the world excluding the United States.

Second, there is strong evidence to suggest that a significant share of the growing level of imports (and hence U.S. trade deficit) from China is coming from export-oriented multinational companies (including U.S. firms[24]) that have moved their production facilities to China to take advantage of China's abundant low-cost labor (among other factors). Chinese data indicate that the share of China's exports produced by foreign-invested enterprises (FIEs) in China has risen dramatically over the past several years. As indicated in Table 3, in 1986, only 1.9% of China's exports were from FIEs, but by 1996, this share had risen to 40.7% and by 2004 it had risen to 57%. A similar pattern can be seen with imports: FIEs accounted for only

5.6% of China's imports in 1986, rose to 47.9% by 2000, and to 58.0% in 2004.

The sharp rise in the share of China's trade by FIEs appears to be strongly linked to the rapid growth in foreign direct investment (FDI) in China, which grew from $1.9 billion in 1986 to $64.0 billion in 2004, much of which went to export-oriented manufacturing, a large share of which was exported to the United States.[25] Data in Table 3 indicate that the U.S. trade deficit with China began to increase rapidly beginning in the early 1990s, roughly the same time that saw a significant rise in FDI in China and a sharp rise in exports by FIEs. By comparing exports and imports in Table 3, one can see that FIEs have little effect on China's overall trade balance, since the FIEs import roughly as much as they export.

Table 3. Exports and Imports by Foreign-Invested Enterprises in China: 1986-2004

| | FDI in China | Exports by FIE | | Imports by FIEs | | U.S. Trade Deficit With China |
	$ billions	$ billions	As a % of Total Chinese Exports	$ billions	As a % of Total Chinese Imports	($ billions)
1986	1.9	$0.6	1.9%	$2.4	5.6%	-$1.7
1987	2.3	1.2	3.1	3.4	7.8	-2.8
1988	3.2	2.5	5.2	5.9	10.6	-3.5
1989	3.4	4.9	9.4	8.8	19.9	-6.2
1990	3.5	7.8	12.6	12.3	23.1	-10.4
1991	4.4	12.0	16.8	16.9	36.5	-12.7
1992	11.0	17.4	20.4	26.4	32.7	-18.2
1993	27.5	25.2	27.5	41.8	40.2	-22.8
1994	33.8	34.7	28.7	52.9	45.8	-29.5
1995	37.5	46.9	31.5	62.9	47.7	-33.8
1996	41.7	61.5	40.7	75.6	54.5	-39.5
1997	45.3	74.9	41.0	77.7	54.6	-49.7
1998	45.4	81.0	44.1	76.7	54.7	-56.9
1999	40.3	88.6	45.5	85.9	51.8	-68.7
2000	40.7	119.4	47.9	117.2	52.1	-83.8
2001	46.9	133.2	50.0	125.8	51.6	-83.1
2002	52.7	169.9	52.2	160.3	54.3	-103.1
2003	53.5	240.3	54.8	231.9	56.0	-124.0
2004	64.0	338.2	57.0	305.6	58.0	-162.0

Source: China's Customs Statistics and U.S. International Trade Commission Dataweb.

FIEs import raw materials and components (much of which come from East Asia) for assembly in China. As a result, China tends to run trade deficits with East Asian countries and trade surpluses with countries with high consumer demand, such as the United States.[26] These factors have led many analysts to conclude that much of the increase in U.S. imports (and hence, the rising U.S. trade deficit with China) is a result of China becoming a production platform for many foreign companies, (who are the largest benefactors from this arrangement) rather than unfair Chinese trade policies.[27] This suggests a fundamental change in trade between China and the United States that could affect the bilateral trade deficit independently of the exchange rate regime.

Table 4. Major Foreign Suppliers of U.S. Computer Equipment Imports: 2000-2004 (billions of $ and % change)

	2000	2001	2002	2003	2004	2000-2004 % Change
Total	68.5	59.0	62.3	64.0	73.9	7.9
China	8.3	8.2	12.0	18.7	29.5	255.4
Malaysia	4.9	5/0	7.1	8.0	8.7	77.6
Mexico	6.9	8.5	7.9	7.0	7.4	7.2
Singapore	8.7	7.1	7.1	6.9	6.6	-24.1
Japan	13.4	9.5	8.1	6.3	6.3	-53.0
Taiwan	8.3	7.0	7.1	5.4	4.1	-50.6

Source: U.S. International Trade Commission Trade Data Web.
Note: Ranked according to top 6 suppliers in 2004.

U.S. trade data strongly suggest that the sharp increase in U.S. imports from China is largely the result of movement in production facilities from other Asian countries to China.[28] That is, various products that used to be made in Japan, Taiwan, Hong Kong, etc., and then exported to the United States are now being made in China (in many cases, by foreign firms in China) and exported to the United States. An illustration of this phenomenon can be seen in Table 4 on U.S. imports of computer equipment and parts from 2000-2004. In 2000, Japan was the largest foreign supplier of U.S. computer equipment (with a 19.6% share of total shipments), while China ranked 4th (at 12.1%). In just five years, Japan's ranking fell to 5th, the value of its shipments dropped by over half, and its share of shipments declined to 8.5% (2004); Singapore and Taiwan also experienced significant declines in their computer equipment shipments to the United States over this period. In 2004, China was by far the largest foreign supplier of computer equipment with a 39.9% share of total shipments. However, while U.S. imports of computer equipment from China rose by 255% over the past five years, the total value of U.S. imports of these commodities rose by only 7.9%, indicating in part that several foreign firms have shifted their production facilities to China.

Third, productivity gains in Chinese exporting firms have increased rapidly in the past few years, a boost to exports that is unrelated to the fixed exchange rate. For example, Chinese export prices have fallen by a cumulative 27% since 1995 in Chinese prices.

Table 5. Percentage Annual Change in U.S. Exports to Top Ten U.S. Export Markets: 2000-2003

Year	2000	2001	2002	2003	2004	2000-2004 Overall Change
Canada	7.6	-7.2	-1.8	5.4	10.8	6.4
Mexico	28.3	-9.1	-3.9	-0.1	13.7	-0.8
Japan	13.5	-11.7	-10.8	1.2	4.5	-16.7
United Kingdom	8.5	-1.9	-18.5	1.9	6.1	-13.1
China	23.9	18.4	14.6	28.9	22.2	112.9
Germany	9.2	3.0	-11.6	8.3	8.8	7.5
South Korea	21.6	-20.4	1.8	6.7	9.3	-5.7
Netherlands	13.2	-11.1	-6.1	12.9	17.3	10.5
Taiwan	27.5	-25.5	1.3	-11.7	24.3	-11.1
France	7.5	-1.8	-4.4	-10.3	24.4	4.4
The World	12.6	-6.3	-5.2	4.4	12.8	4.6

Source: United States International Trade Commission *Dataweb*.
Note: Listed according to the top 10 U.S. export markets in 2004.

Fourth, the sharp rise in the U.S. trade deficit with China diverts attention from the fact that, while U.S. imports from China have been rising rapidly, U.S. exports to China have been increasing sharply as well. Table 5 lists annual percentage change in U.S. exports to its top 10 trading partners and to the world for the period 2000-2004. These data indicate that U.S. exports to China have risen more sharply than total U.S. exports to the world and more than any other top 10 U.S. trading partners. China was one of the only significant export markets that has grown during the world wide economic downturn in 2001 and 2002. During this period, total U.S. exports declined by 6.3% and 5.2%, while U.S. exports to China rose by 18.4% and 14.6%, respectively. In 2004, total U.S. exports rose by 12.8%, while those to China rose by 22.2%. From 2000-2004, total U.S. exports rose by 4.6%, while those to China grew by 112.9%. China also went from being the 11th largest U.S. export market in 2000 to its 5th largest market in 2004.[29] China's rapid economic growth and implementation of its WTO commitments is likely to result in continued rapid growth in U.S. exports to China.[30]

ECONOMIC CONSEQUENCES OF CHINA'S CURRENCY PEG

If the yuan is undervalued against the dollar, as many critics charge, then there are benefits and costs of this policy for the economies of both China and the United States.

Implications of the Peg for China's Economy

If the yuan is undervalued, then Chinese exports to the United States are likely cheaper than they would be if the currency were freely traded, providing a boost to China's export industries (which employ millions of workers and are a major source of China's productivity gains). Eliminating exchange rate risk through a peg also increases the attractiveness of China as a destination for foreign investment in export-oriented production facilities, much of which comes from U.S. firms. However, an undervalued currency makes imports more expensive, hurting Chinese consumers and Chinese firms that import parts, machinery, and raw materials. Such a policy, in effect, benefits Chinese exporting firms (many of which are owned by foreign multinational corporations) at the expense of non-exporting Chinese firms, especially those that rely on imported goods. This may impede the most efficient allocation of resources in the Chinese economy.

The accumulation of large foreign exchange reserves by China may make it easier for Chinese officials to move more quickly toward adopting a fully convertible currency (if the government feels it could defend the currency against speculative pressures). However, the accumulation of large foreign exchange reserves (which reached $610 billion in December 2004) also entails opportunity costs for China: such funds (instead of sitting in the central bank) could be used to fund China's massive development needs, such as infrastructure improvements, that may have a higher rate of return than U.S. Treasuries.

Implications of the Peg for the U.S. Economy

Effect on Exporters and Import-Competitors

When a fixed exchange rate causes the yuan to be less expensive than it would be if it were floating, it causes Chinese exports to the United States to be relatively inexpensive and U.S. exports to China to be relatively expensive. As a result, U.S. exports and the production of U.S. goods and services that compete with Chinese imports fall, in the short run.[31] Many of the affected firms are in the manufacturing sector, as will be discussed below. This causes the U.S. trade deficit to rise and reduces aggregate demand in the short run, all else equal.[32]

China has become the United States's second largest supplier of imports (2004 data). A large share of China's exports to the United States are labor-intensive consumer goods, such as toys and games, textiles and apparel, shoes, and consumer electronics. Many of these products do not compete directly with U.S. domestic producers — the manufacture of many such products shifted overseas several years ago. However, there are a number of U.S. industries (many of which are small and medium-sized firms), including makers of machine tools, hardware, plastics, furniture, and tool and die that are expressing concern over the growing competitive challenge posed by China.[33] An undervalued Chinese currency may contribute to a reduction in the output of such industries.

On the other hand, U.S. producers also import capital equipment and inputs to final products from China. For example, U.S. computer firms use a significant level of imported computer parts in their production, and China was the largest foreign supplier of computer equipment to the United States in 2004. An undervalued yuan lowers the price of these U.S. products, increasing their output and competitiveness in world markets. And many imports from China are produced by U.S.-invested enterprises (as discussed above), which benefit from an undervalued peg.

Effect on U.S. Borrowers

An undervalued yuan also has an effect on U.S. borrowers. When the United States runs a current account deficit with China, an equivalent amount of capital flows from China to the United States, as can be seen in the U.S. balance of payments accounts. This occurs because the Chinese central bank or private Chinese citizens are investing in U.S. assets, which allows more U.S. capital investment in plant and equipment to take place than would otherwise occur. Capital investment increases because the greater demand for U.S. assets puts downward pressure on U.S. interest rates, and firms are now willing to make investments that were previously unprofitable. This increases aggregate spending in the short run, all else equal, and also increases the size of the economy in the long run by increasing the capital stock.

Private firms are not the only beneficiaries of the lower interest rates caused by the capital inflow (trade deficit) from China. Interest-sensitive household spending, on goods such as consumer durables and housing, is also higher than it would be if capital from China did not flow into the United States. In addition, a large proportion of the U.S. assets bought by the Chinese, particularly by the central bank, are U.S. Treasury securities, which fund U.S. federal budget deficits. According to the U.S. Treasury Department, China (as of January 2005) held $194.5 billion in U.S. Treasury securities, making China the second largest foreign holder of such securities (after Japan). If the U.S. trade deficit with China were eliminated, Chinese capital would no longer flow into this country on net, and the government would have to find other buyers of its U.S. Treasuries. This would increase the government's interest payments, increasing the budget deficit, all else equal.

Effect on U.S. Consumers

A society's economic well-being is usually measured not by how much it can produce, but how much it can consume. An undervalued yuan that lowers the price of imports from China allows the United States to increase its consumption of both imported and domestically produced goods through an improvement in the terms-of-trade. The terms-of-trade measures the terms on which U.S. labor and capital can be exchanged for foreign labor and capital. Since changes in aggregate spending are only temporary, from a long-term perspective the lasting effect of an undervalued yuan is to increase the purchasing power of U.S. consumers.[34]

U.S.-China Trade and Manufacturing Jobs

Critics of China's currency peg argue that the low value of the yuan has had a significant effect on the U.S. manufacturing sector, where 2.7 million factory jobs have been lost since July 2000. While job losses in the U.S. manufacturing sector have been significant in recent years, there is no clear link between job losses and imports from China. First, only some manufacturers export to China or compete with Chinese imports. Second, the economic recession and subsequent "jobless recovery" that ended in August 2003 reduced employment across the entire economy. Third, the "strong dollar" and growing trade deficit have not been limited to China; the trade-weighted dollar index was appreciating until early 2002 and the overall trade deficit is still increasing.

Finally, there is a long-run trend that is moving U.S. production away from manufacturing and toward the service sector.[35] U.S. employment in manufacturing as a share of total nonagricultural employment has fallen from 31.8% in 1960 to 22.4% in 1980 to 12.8% in 2002.[36] This trend is much larger than the Chinese currency issue, and is caused by changing technology (which requires fewer workers to produce the same number of goods)[37] and comparative advantage. With enhanced globalization, comparative advantage predicts the United States will produce knowledge- and technology-intensive goods that it is best at producing for trade with countries, such as China, who are better at producing labor-intensive goods. Since the production of some manufactured goods is labor-intensive and some services cannot be traded, trade leads to more manufacturing abroad, and less in the United States.[38] Over time, it is likely that the trend shifting manufacturing abroad will continue regardless of China's currency peg.

The decline in manufacturing employment is not unique to the United States. According to a study by Alliance Capital Management, employment in manufacturing among the world's 20 largest economies declined by 22 million jobs between 1995 and 2002. At the same time, the study estimated that total manufacturing production among these economies increased by more than 30% (due largely to increases in productivity). As indicated in Table 6, while the number of manufacturing jobs in the United States declined by 1.9 million (or 11.3%) during this period, they declined in many other industrial countries as well, including Japan (2.3 million or 16.1%), Germany (476,000 or 10.1%), the United Kingdom (446,000 or 10.3%), and South Korea (555,000 or 11.6%). The study further estimated employment in manufacturing in China during this period declined by 15 million workers (from 96 million workers in 1995 to 83 million in 2002), a 15.3% reduction.[39] In the United States and United Kingdom, the employment decline began in 1999; in the other countries in Table 6, the decline began earlier. In 2004, the industrialized countries experienced a loss of 865,000 more manufacturing jobs, and a cumulative 6.3 million manufacturing job losses over the previous five years.[40]

The sharp increases in U.S. imports of manufactured products from China over the past several years do not necessarily correlate with subsequent production and job losses in the manufacturing sector. A study by the Federal Reserve Bank of Chicago estimated that the import penetration by Chinese manufactured products (i.e., the ratio of imported manufactured Chinese goods to total manufactured goods consumed domestically) was only 2.7% in 2001.[41] The study acknowledged that, while China on average is a small-to-moderate player in most manufacturing sector markets in the United States, it has shown a high growth in import penetration over the past few years, growing by nearly 60% between 1997-2001 (from 1.7% to 2.7%). However, the study concluded that "the bulk of the current U.S. manufacturing weakness cannot be attributed to rising imports and outsourcing," but rather is largely the result of the economic slowdown in the United States and among several major U.S. export markets.[42]

Table 6. Manufacturing Employment in Selected Countries: 1995 and 2002
(in thousands and percent change)

	Manufacturing Employment (000)		Change in Manufacturing Employment: 1995/2002	
	1995	2002	Total Change (000)	Percent Change (%)
United States	17,251	15,304	-1,947	-11.3
Japan	14,570	12,230	-2,340	-16.1
Germany	8,439	7,963	-476	-10.1
United Kingdom	4,402	3,956	-446	-10.3
South Korea	4,796	4,241	-555	-11.6
China	98,030	83,080	-14,950	-15.3

Source: Alliance Capital Management L.P., Alliance Bernstein, *Manufacturing Payrolls Declining Globally: The Untold Story*, U.S. Weekly Economic Update, October 10, 2003.

Determining how much of the loss in manufacturing employment is due to Chinese imports would require sophisticated economic modeling, and is beyond the scope of this report. But by making a simple calculation, an upper-bound estimate can be placed on how much manufacturing job loss can be attributable to Chinese imports to put the issue in perspective. If imports have a one-time effect on U.S. employment, then the relevant figure is the increase in (not the level of) Chinese imports over the past couple of years. Between 2000 and 2002, manufacturing imports from Chinese increased by about $25 billion. At the same time, U.S. manufacturing exports to China increased by $5 billion. If we assumed that every additional dollar of Chinese manufacturing imports reduced US manufacturing output by one dollar - a highly unrealistic assumption - and every additional dollar of manufacturing exports increased manufacturing output, then trade with

China can account for about a 1.5%, or 0.25 million, decline in manufacturing employment from 2000 to 2002. Manufacturing employment fell by 11.3%, or 2 million, from 2000-2002, so that trade with China can only explain at most about one eighth of the total decline in those years. The Chicago Fed study cites two reasons why the actual figure would be smaller:

- the positive economic effects of low-priced Chinese goods on real incomes in the United States (which enables consumers to purchase more goods and services, including those from domestic sources); and
- the fact that many such products, if they were not made in China, would be imported from other foreign countries.

In addition, the actual job loss would be smaller because of the expansion in output of interest-sensitive industries, which include some manufacturing industries, since the capital inflow from China lowers U.S. interest rates.

Net Effect on the U.S. Economy

In the medium run, an undervalued yuan neither increases nor decreases aggregate demand in the United States. Rather, it leads to a compositional shift in U.S. production, away from U.S. exporters and import-competing firms toward the firms that benefit from the lower interest rates caused by Chinese capital inflows. In particular, capital-intensive firms and firms that produce consumer durables would be expected to benefit from lower interest rates. Thus, it is expected to have no medium- or long-run effect on aggregate U.S. employment or unemployment. As evidence, one can consider that the United States had a historically large and growing trade deficit throughout the 1990s at a time when unemployment reached a three-decade low and there was no decline in manufacturing employment. However, the gains and losses in employment and production caused by the trade deficit will not be dispersed evenly across regions and sectors of the economy: on balance, some areas will gain while others will lose.

Although the compositional shift in output has no negative effect on aggregate U.S. output and employment in the long-run, there may be adverse short-run consequences. If output in the trade sector falls more quickly than the output of U.S. recipients of Chinese capital rises, aggregate spending and employment could temporarily fall. If this occurs, then there is likely to be a decline in the inflation rate as well (which could be beneficial or harmful, depending if inflation is high or low at the time). A fall in aggregate spending is more likely to be a concern if the economy is already sluggish than if it is at full employment. Otherwise, it is likely that government macroeconomic policy adjustment and market forces can quickly compensate for any decline of output in the trade sector by expanding other elements of aggregate demand.

By shifting the composition of U.S. output to a higher capital base, the size of the economy would be larger in the long run as a result of the capital inflow/trade deficit. U.S. citizens would not enjoy the returns to Chinese-owned capital in the United States. U.S. workers employing that Chinese-owned capital would enjoy higher productivity, however, and correspondingly higher wages.

The U.S.-China Trade Deficit in the Context of the Overall U.S. Trade Deficit

While China is a large trading partner, it accounted for only about 13.4% of U.S. imports in 2004 and 23.0% of the sum of the bilateral trade deficits. Over a span of several years, a country with a floating exchange rate can run an ongoing overall trade deficit for only one reason: a domestic imbalance between saving and investment. This has been the case for the United States over the past two decades, where saving as a share of gross domestic product (GDP) has been in gradual decline.[43] On the one hand, the United States has high rates of productivity growth and strong economic fundamentals that are conducive to high rates of capital investment. On the other hand, it has a chronically low household saving rate, and recently a negative government saving rate as a result of the budget deficit. As long as Americans save little, foreigners will use their saving to finance profitable investment opportunities in the United States; the trade deficit is the result.[44] The returns to foreign-owned capital will flow to foreigners instead of Americans, but the returns to U.S. labor utilizing foreign-owned capital will flow to U.S. labor.

For this reason, economists generally are more concerned with the overall trade deficit than bilateral trade balances. Because of comparative advantage, it is natural that a country will have some trading partners from which it imports more, and some trading partners to which it exports more. For example, the United States has a trade deficit with Austria and a trade surplus with the Netherlands even though both countries use the euro, which floats against the dollar. Of concern to the United States from an economic perspective is that its low saving rate makes it so reliant on foreigners to finance its investment opportunities, and not the fact that much of the capital comes from China.[45] If the United States did not borrow from China as a result of the exchange rate peg, it would still have to borrow from other countries.[46]

POLICY OPTIONS FOR THE PEG AND U.S. TRADE POLICY WITH CHINA

The United States could utilize a number of options to try to induce China to change its exchange rate policy if U.S. policymakers deemed that such a policy would promote overall U.S. economic interests.[47] Options for currency reform range from making the yuan fully convertible to keeping the peg but revaluing the yuan against the dollar by a certain amount to switching to a peg against a basket of international currencies.[48] Options to induce China to reform its exchange rate regime might include (1) diplomatic efforts to convince China to change the peg; (2) utilization of U.S. trade laws (such as Section 301 of the 1974 Trade Act, as amended, used to respond to unfair foreign trade barriers), which might involve the threat of imposing unilateral trade sanctions against China; and (3) trying to make a case before the World Trade Organization (WTO) that China's currency peg violates multilateral trade rules.

Changes to the Peg and Potential Outcomes

If the Chinese were to allow their currency to float, its value would be determined by private actors in the market based on the supply and demand for Chinese goods and assets relative to U.S. goods and assets. If the relative demand for the Chinese currency has increased since the exchange rate was fixed in 1994, then the floating currency would appreciate. This would boost U.S. exports and the output of U.S. producers who compete with the Chinese. The U.S. bilateral trade deficit would likely decline (but not necessarily disappear). At the same time, the Chinese central bank would no longer purchase U.S. assets to maintain the peg. U.S. borrowers, including the federal government, would now need to find new lenders to finance their borrowing, and interest rates in the United States would rise. This would reduce spending on interest-sensitive purchases, such as capital investment, housing (residential investment), and consumer durables. The reduction in investment spending would reduce the long-run size of the U.S. economy. If the relative demand for Chinese goods and assets were to fall at some point in the future, the floating exchange rate would depreciate, and the effects would be reversed. Floating exchange rates fluctuate in value frequently and significantly.[49] Over time, the volatility of the floating rate could reduce the levels of bilateral trade and investment between the United States and China.

A move to a floating exchange rate is typically accompanied by the elimination of capital controls that limit a country's private citizens from freely purchasing and selling foreign currency. Capital controls exist in China today, and one of the major reasons China arguably opposes a floating exchange rate is because it fears that the removal of capital controls would lead to a large private capital outflow from China. This might occur because Chinese citizens fear that their deposits in the potentially insolvent state banking system are unsafe. If the capital outflow were large enough, it could cause the floating exchange rate to depreciate rather than appreciate.[50] If this occurred, the output of U.S. exporters and import-competing firms would be reduced below the level prevailing under the fixed exchange rate regime, and the U.S. bilateral trade deficit would expand. In other words, the United States would still borrow heavily from China, but it would now be private citizens buying U.S. assets instead of the Chinese central bank. China could attempt to float its exchange rate while maintaining its capital controls, at least temporarily. This solution would eliminate the possibility that the currency would depreciate because of a private capital outflow. While this would be unusual, it might be possible. It would likely make it more difficult to impose effective capital controls, however, since the fluctuating currency would offer a much greater profit incentive for evasion.

If the Chinese were to revalue their currency (adjusting the peg) to the rate that would prevail in the market, the immediate effects on the U.S. economy would be the same as if the yuan were allowed to float: it would increase the output of exporters and import-competing firms and reduce interest-sensitive U.S. spending. The difference between revaluation and floating would occur over time. With future changes in the relative demand for goods and assets, the yuan could again become overvalued or undervalued. If it were to become overvalued, it could come under speculative attack, as happened to Southeast Asian currencies during the Asian Crisis, since investors would view the government as more willing to alter the exchange rate. Revaluing would have the advantage of maintaining exchange rate stability, which would lead to closer bilateral trade and investment ties than if the yuan were allowed to float. (Revaluing would lead to lower bilateral trade and investment flows compared to maintaining a constant peg, however, since the peg would now be viewed as less permanent.) China would also be able to maintain its capital controls, preventing the possibility of a destabilizing capital outflow by its private citizens.[51]

Another option is to maintain the status quo. Although the nominal exchange rate would stay constant in this case, over time the real rate would adjust as inflation rates in the two countries diverged. As the central bank exchanged newly printed yuan for U.S. assets, prices in China would rise along with the money supply until the real exchange rate was brought back into line with the market rate. This would cause the U.S. bilateral trade deficit to decline and expand the output of U.S. exporters and import-competing firms. This real exchange rate adjustment would only occur over time, however, and pressures on the U.S. trade sector would persist in the meantime.

None of the solutions guarantee that the bilateral trade deficit will be eliminated. China is a country with a high saving rate, and the United States is a country with a low saving rate; it is natural that their overall trade balance would be in surplus and deficit, respectively. At the bilateral level, it is not unusual for two countries to run persistently imbalanced trade, even with a floating exchange rate. If China can continue its combination of low-cost labor and rapid productivity gains, which have been reducing export prices in yuan terms, its exports to the United States are likely to continue to grow regardless of the exchange rate regime.

Policy Options to Induce China to Reform the Peg

Diplomatic Efforts

The U.S. government could attempt to persuade China through direct negotiations to change or reform its exchange rate policy. President Bush on a number of occasions has criticized China's currency peg, stating that exchange rates should be determined by market forces, and he raised the issue in a meeting with Chinese President Hu Jintao in October 2003. Shortly before that meeting, the United States was able to convince China to agree to the establishment of a joint technical cooperation program to promote the development of China's financial markets and to examine ways China can move more quickly toward a floating exchange rate.[52] Alternatively, the United States could attempt to persuade China to participate in talks with other East Asian economies (that are viewed as intervening in currency markets) in order to reach a consensus on exchange rate policy.[53] A key factor in any negotiations would be to convince China that liberalization of its exchange rate system would serve China's long term economic interests.

Utilize Section 301

The U.S. government could attempt to pressure China by threatening to impose unilateral trade sanctions. For example, it could threaten to initiate a *Section 301* case, a provision in U.S. trade law that gives the U.S. Trade Representative authority to respond to foreign trade barriers, including violations of U.S. rights under a trade agreement, and unreasonable or discriminatory practices that burden or restrict U.S. commerce.[54] If the United States contended that China's currency peg violated WTO rules (see below), it would then have to bring a dispute settlement proceeding before the WTO. If the United States contended that China's currency policy was not covered under WTO agreements and burdened or restricted U.S. trade, it could then proceed under the Section 301 mechanism. This would involve negotiations with China to remove the trade barrier within a specified time period, and potentially, the imposition of trade sanctions against China (such as higher tariffs on Chinese goods imported into the United States) if the issue could not be resolved. However, China might respond with sanctions against U.S. products, or it could bring a case against the United States in the WTO, arguing that U.S. sanctions against China violated WTO trade rules.

Utilize the Dispute Resolution Mechanism in the WTO

Some critics have charged that China's currency policy violates WTO rules.[55] The United States could file a case before the WTO's Dispute Settlement Body (DSB) against China's currency peg.[56] If the DSB ruled in favor of the United States, it would direct China to modify its currency policy so that it complies with WTO rules. If China refused to comply, the DSB would likely authorize the United States to impose trade sanctions against China. The advantage of using the WTO to resolve the issue is that it involves a multilateral, rather than unilateral, approach, although there is no guarantee that the WTO would rule in favor of the United States.[57]

In 2004, the Bush Administration rejected two Section 301 petitions on China's exchange rate policy: one by the the China Currency Coalition (a group of U.S. industrial, service, agricultural, and labor organizations) and one filed by 30 Members of Congress. Both petitions sought to have the United States bring a case before the WTO against China in the hope that the WTO would rule that China's currency peg violated WTO rules. The Bush Administration has expressed doubts that the United States could win such a case in the WTO and contends that such an approach would be "more damaging than helpful at this time."[58]

Utilize Special Safeguard Measures

Another option might be to utilize U.S. trade remedy laws relating to special provisions that were part of China's accession to the WTO. For example, the United States could invoke safeguard provisions (under Sections 421-423 of the 1974 Trade Act, as amended) to impose restrictions on imported Chinese products that have increased in such quantities that they have caused, or threaten to cause, market disruption to U.S. domestic producers.[59] This option could be used to provide temporary relief for U.S. domestic firms that have been negatively affected by a surge in Chinese exports to the United States (regardless of its cause).[60] Broadly speaking, any imposed U.S. trade restrictions of Chinese goods would likely reduce overall U.S. economic welfare, because the reduction in the welfare of U.S. consumers (as import prices rise) would likely exceed the increase in welfare of U.S. producers.

Other Bilateral Commercial Issues

A number of policy analysts have argued against pushing China too hard on the peg, either because it would not serve U.S. economic interests, or because U.S. pressure would likely be ineffective as long as the Chinese government believed changing the peg would damage China's economy.[61] Such analysts argue that U.S. policymakers should address China's currency peg as part of a more comprehensive U.S. trade strategy to persuade China to accelerate economic and trade reforms and to address a wide range of U.S. complaints over China's trade practices. Many U.S. firms and policymakers have expressed disappointment with China's record on WTO implementation. In a speech before the American Chamber of Commerce in Beijing on October 28, 2003, then U.S. Commerce Secretary Don Evans stated that U.S. patience on China's WTO compliance was "wearing thin" and warned of "growing protectionist sentiments" in the United States against China. Major WTO-related issues of concern to the United States include market access, inadequate protection of U.S. intellectual property rights (IPR), tax rebates for certain exporting industries, and indirect subsidization of Chinese state-owned enterprises by China's banking system.

- **Market Access Issues**. U.S. officials have been critical of Chinese policies that have prevented U.S. firms from gaining market access promised under China's WTO commitments. Major policies affecting market access include the administration of tariff rates and quotas, health and safety regulations on agricultural products, excessive capitalization requirements for foreign providers of services, restrictions on trading and distribution rights, continued technology transfer requirements on U.S. joint ventures in China, and insufficient regulatory transparency.
- **IPR**. Under the terms of its WTO accession, China agreed immediately to bring its IPR laws in compliance with the WTO agreement on Trade Related Aspects of Intellectual Property Rights (TRIPS). U.S. business groups continue to experience significant IPR problems in China, especially in terms of illegal reproduction of software, retail piracy, and trademark counterfeiting. It is estimated that counterfeits account for 15 to 20% of all products made in China. Chinese enforcement agencies and judicial system often lack the resources (or the will) needed to vigorously enforce IPR laws; convicted IPR offenders generally face minor penalties. In addition, while market access for IPR-related products has improved, high tariffs, quotas, and other barriers continue to hamper U.S. exports; such trade barriers are believed to be partly responsible for illegal IPR-related smuggling and counterfeiting in China. Industry analysts estimate that IPR piracy in China cost U.S. firms $2.5 billion in lost sales in 2004. The piracy rate for IPR-related products in China (such as motion pictures, software, and sound recordings) is estimated at around 90%.[62]
- **Tax Rebates**. The Chinese government has attempted to use tax rebates (since 1985) to promote the development of certain export industries and to provide temporary relief to firms during economic slowdowns.[63] U.S. firms have argued that this policy is unfair and a violation of WTO rules because it provides a de facto subsidy to exporting firms in China and because it discriminates against imported products (which are not eligible for the tax rebates). For example, the value-added tax on imported semiconductors is 17%. Tax rebates are given to domestic producers of semiconductors, such that chips made in China are assessed a VAT rate of 6% and chips designed and made in China pay a 3% VAT.[64] According to Chinese government figures, export tax rebates totaled $29.8 billion in 2002.[65] In October 2003, the Chinese government announced plans to roll back

the average rebate on its export tax by an average of three percentage points.[66]

- **Industry Subsidies**. Another major concern to U.S. businesses is the Chinese government's continued financial assistance to its state-owned enterprises (SOEs). Although China agreed to make SOEs operate according to free market principles when it joined the WTO, U.S. officials contend that such enterprises are still being heavily subsidized through the banking system.[67] This is seen as a significant problem since nearly half of China's exports come from SOEs. The use of subsidies is viewed as giving Chinese firms an unfair trade advantage.

Many analysts contend that an intensified effort toward inducing China to fully comply with its WTO commitments could result in substantial new trade and investment opportunities for U.S. firms, and hence could help reduce trade tensions between the two countries. In addition, because China's WTO commitments are clear and binding, and there is a legal process within the WTO to seek compliance with trade agreements, the United States is in a stronger position to get China to liberalize its economy and open its markets than it would be if it tried to push China to reform its currency regime (where multilateral rules and options on the issue are less clear). Finally, supporters of this policy argue that China's leaders are more likely to respond to pressures to adhere to international rules of conduct than to perceived direct U.S. pressure.

Legislation in the 109th Congress

Eleven bills were introduced in the 108th that sought to address China's currency policy or to take action against countries that "manipulated" their exchange rates. A number of bills have been introduced in the 109th Congress to address the currency issue.

- S. 14 (Stabenow), S. 295 (Schumer), and H.R. 1575 (Spratt) directs the Secretary of the Treasury to negotiate with China to accept a market-based system of currency valuation, and imposes an additional duty of 27.5% on Chinese goods imported into the United States unless the President submits a certification to Congress that China is no longer manipulating the rate of exchange and is complying with accepted market-based trading policies.

- S. 377 (Lieberman) directs the President to negotiate with those countries determined to be engaged most egregiously in currency manipulation and to seek an end to such manipulation. If an agreement is not reached, the President is directed to institute proceedings under the relevant U.S. and international trade laws and to seek appropriate damages and remedies for the U.S. manufacturers and other affected parties.

On April 6, 2005, the Senate failed (by a vote of 33 to 67) to table an amendment, S.Amdt. 309 (Schumer) to S. 600 (Foreign Affairs Authorization Act), which would impose a 27.5% tariff on Chinese goods if China failed to substantially appreciate its currency to market levels. In response to the vote, the Senate leadership moved to allow a vote on S. 295 (which has same language as S.Amdt. 309) no later than July 27, 2005 as long as the sponsors of the amendment agree not to sponsor similar amendments for the duration of the 109th Congress.

Opponents of legislation that would imposed additional tariffs against China for not appreciating its currency charge that it would violate WTO rules. Many analysts contend that China's currency peg violates a number of WTO provisions and have urged the Bush Administration to initiate a WTO dispute resolution case against China. On April 20, 2005, a coalition of 35 Members of Congress filed a Section 301 case with the USTR calling on the United States to bring a trade dispute case against China in the WTO over its currency peg policy.

Some Members of Congress support changing U.S. law to apply countervailing laws to nonmarket economies so that U.S. firms are able to take action against unfair government subsidies, especially in regards to China. They further contend that China's currency peg constitutes a government exports subsidy that should be actionable under U.S. countervailing laws. H.R. 1216 (English) and S. 593 (Collins) would apply U.S. countervailing laws to nonmarket economies. H.R. 1498 (Tim Ryan) would apply U.S. countervailing laws to countries that manipulate their currencies.

CONCLUSION

The current debate among U.S. policymakers over China's currency peg has been strongly linked to concerns over the growing U.S. trade deficit with China, the sharp decline in U.S. manufacturing employment over the past few years, and the rise of China as a major economic power. Most economists agree that China's currency would appreciate against the dollar if allowed to float. If it did, there is considerable debate over the net effects this policy would have on the U.S. economy since it may benefit some U.S. economic sectors and harm other sectors, as well as consumers. In addition, U.S. trade with China is only one of a number of factors affecting manufacturing employment, including increased productivity growth, employment shifts to the service sector, and the overall trade deficit. It is also not clear to what extent production in certain industrial sectors has shifted to China from the United States, as opposed to shifting to China from other low-wage countries, such as Mexico, Thailand, and Indonesia.[68] The extensive involvement of foreign multilateral corporations in China's manufactured exports further complicates the issue of who really benefits from China's trade, as well as the implications of a rising U.S. trade deficit with China (since a large share of U.S. imports are coming from foreign firms, including U.S. firms, that have shifted production from one country to China). Thus, there is considerable debate over what policy options would promote U.S. economic interests since changes to the current system would produce both winners and losers in the United States (as well as in China).

Chinese officials are reluctant to change their currency peg, largely because it has facilitated economic stability, a contributing factor to China's rapid economic growth over the past several years. Such growth has substantially raised living standards and reduced poverty. The World Bank estimates that Chinese economic reforms have helped lift 402 million people out of poverty (based on a $1 per day expenditure level). However, as of 2002, there were still 88 million Chinese living in poverty.[69] China, like many other developing countries, is largely relying on exporting as a key factor in its economic growth and employment strategy, especially as it attempts to scale back the involvement of SOEs in the economy. Chinese leaders (and many foreign economists) contend that, given the poor state of China's banking system, a move toward a fully convertible currency could spark an economic crisis in China, and could even cause the yuan to depreciate if there were a loss of confidence in the banking system. At the same time, however, maintaining the peg likely entails a number of costs to the Chinese economy. Thus, in the long run, it is in China's own economic interests to reform its banking system and move towards a fully convertible currency in order to ensure the most efficient allocation of resources within the economy. However, it is unclear how quickly China can achieve these two goals.

Much of the debate over China's peg is linked to the question of how China's economic development is affecting, or will affect, U.S. economic interests.[70] In the past, most U.S.-China trade was considered complementary, that is, most of the goods the United States imported from China were consumer-oriented, labor intensive products that were no longer being produced in the United States. In recent years, an increasing level of U.S. imports have been advanced technology products. China has made it a top priority to develop a number of industries, such as computers and autos, which has raised concerns that the United States faces a "competitive threat" from China similar to the perceived "competitive threat" the rise of the Japanese economy in the 1970s and 1980s posed to several U.S. economic sectors. The divergent experience of the U.S. and Japanese economies since the 1990s suggests that the competitive threat from China is questionable. In the long run, China's economic development and exchange rate regime poses little threat to America's ability to achieve healthy economic growth and full employment.

A rapidly growing and modernizing Chinese economy would be detrimental to the United States economically if the United States experienced a significant decline in its terms-of-trade (the terms on which U.S. labor and capital can be exchanged for Chinese labor and capital).[71] However, a case can be made that the terms-of-trade would move in favor of the United States as China develops since Chinese markets for many of the products the U.S. specializes in producing (e.g., services, luxury goods) are small now, but would presumably expand as Chinese disposable income continues to rise. According to the World Economic Forum, the United States currently ranks as the world's second most competitive economy (after Finland) in terms of its ability to sustain long-term economic growth (based on a number of factors, such as macroeconomic policy, efficiency of public institutions, and technological development). China ranks 44th out of 102 countries surveyed.[72]

Many argue that, because China is becoming such a large player in the world economy, it must be made to "play by the rules" to ensure a "level playing field" for U.S. firms and to prevent them from being harmed by unfair Chinese trading practices. A major challenge for U.S. policymakers is to pursue macroeconomic and trade policies that promote economic efficiency and maximize the benefits of trade for the U.S. economy.

REFERENCES

[1] A brief summary of this report can be found in CRS Report RS21625, *China's Currency Peg: Implications for the U.S. and Chinese Economies*, by Marc Labonte and Wayne Morrison.

[2] See Prepared Remarks of Dr. C. Fred Bergsten, President, Institute for International Economics, before the House Small Business Committee, June 25, 2003.

[3] The White House, Office of the Press Secretary, Background Briefing by a Senior Administration Official on the President's Meeting with the President of China, Oct. 19, 2003.

[4] Prior to this time, China maintained a dual exchange rate system: an official exchange rate of about 5.8 yuan to the dollar and a market swap rate (used mainly for trade transactions) of about 8.7 yuan to the dollar (at the end of 1993). The reforms in 1994 unified the two rates. Since Hong Kong also fixes its exchange rate to the dollar, China in effect also maintains a fixed exchange rate with Hong Kong.

[5] Only data on overall Chinese foreign reserves are publicly available. Data are not available to determine how much of the increase in foreign reserves comes from the accumulation of assets of other countries (e.g., Japan or the Euro area). If the increase in foreign reserves came from the purchase of non-U.S. assets, the increase would play no role in the defense of the exchange rate peg. By comparing Chinese foreign reserve data to data reported by the U.S. Treasury on total U.S. assets purchased by China (from private and official sources), an upper bound of China's reserves held in U.S. securities is $194.5 billion of U.S. Treasury securities at the end of 2004 and $88 billion of U.S. agency debt in June 2003. Therefore, at least half of the central bank's holdings were not U.S. assets. The upper bound is probably too high since it assumes all U.S. assets were bought by the central bank. Source: U.S. Treasury "Report on Foreign Portfolio Holdings of U.S. Securities," June 2003; U.S. Treasury International Capital System.

[6] If the demand for yuan relative to dollars were to decline, the central bank would face the opposite situation. It would need to buy yuan from the public in exchange for U.S. dollars to maintain the peg. This strategy could only be continued until the central bank's dollar reserves were exhausted, at which point the peg would have to be abandoned.

[7]   Some commentators have suggested that the extent of yuan undervaluation can be estimated from inflation differentials. In other words, although the nominal exchange rate has been constant, adjusting for inflation can determine how much the real rate has depreciated, and proves that the yuan is undervalued. The problem with this approach is that the estimate will be highly sensitive to the selection of the base year. For example, if the base year was 1996, the yuan would have been undervalued by 14% in 2002, but if the base year was 1994, the yuan would have been *overvalued* by 5% in 2002. The current account balance was close to zero (one definition of equilibrium) in both years.

[8]   The Chinese can try to offset the upward pressure on prices by selling Chinese government securities to take the additional yuan out of circulation (called "sterilized intervention"). But this will push interest rates back up, attracting more foreign capital to China, causing the central bank's dollar reserves and the supply of yuan to expand again. It is difficult to tell whether the Chinese have sterilized their foreign reserve accumulation in recent years. All else equal, if China sterilized its intervention, the growth rate of the money supply and the inflation rate would not rise. The growth rate of one measure of the Chinese money supply, M2, accelerated in both 2001 and 2002. The growth rate of another measure, M1, decelerated in 2001 but accelerated in 2002. Inflation was very low through 2003, but rose to 3.9% in 2004. However, inflation and money growth could have been affected by factors other than reserve accumulation in recent years. It has been argued that sterilization is an "unfair" practice to use with a peg, since it is meant to prevent the price adjustment that brings trade between the two countries back into equilibrium.

[9]   For more information, see CRS Report RL31204, *Fixed Exchange Rates, Floating Exchange Rates, and Currency Boards: What Have We Learned?* by Marc Labonte.

[10] For detailed information and a time line on Chinese capital controls, see Eswar Prasad and Shang-Jin Wei, "The Chinese Approach to Capital Inflows: Patterns and Possible Explanations," IMF working paper 05/79, April 2005.

[11] Ernest H. Preeg, "Exchange Rate Manipulation to Gain an Unfair Competitive Advantage: The Case against Japan and China," in C. Fred Bergsten and John Williamson, eds., *Dollar Overvaluation and the World Economy* (Washington, DC: Institute for International Economics, 2003).

[12] According to the data cited elsewhere in this report, the actual surplus in 2002 was 2.9% of GDP and 2.2% in 2003.

[13] Morris Goldstein, testimony before the Subcommittee on Domestic and International Monetary Policy, Committee on Financial Services, U.S. House of Representatives, Oct. 1, 2003.

[14] Jim O'Neill and Dominic Wilson, *How China Can Help the World,* Goldman Sachs Global Economics Paper 97, Sept. 17, 2003.

[15] A thorough attempt to estimate exchange rates according to this method can be found in John Williamson, ed., *Estimating Equilibrium Exchange Rates* (Washington, DC: Institute for International Economics, 1994).

[16] Barry Bosworth, "Valuing the Renminbi," paper presented at Tokyo Club Research Meeting, February 9-10, 2004.

[17] Sensible rules of thumb for long-term sustainability, such as estimating the current account deficit that would keep U.S. assets a constant share of foreign investment portfolios, need not hold in the short run. For instance, after a change in fundamentals, current account deficits may persist for several years as the United States transitions to a new steady state.

[18] On the basis of the data used in this report, the bilateral trade surplus less FDI equaled about $50 billion, rather than $60 billion, in 2002, and China's overall trade balance less FDI equaled a *deficit* of about $15 billion.

[19] Bosworth points out that, by this measure, the Indian rupee is even more undervalued, yet few people make that argument. Bosworth, *Op Cit.*

[20] Jeffrey Frankel, "On the Renminbi: The Choice Between Adjustment Under a Fixed Exchange Rate and Adjustment Under a Flexible Exchange Rate," National Bureau of Economic Research, working paper 11274, April 2005, p. 3.

[21] *Economist,* "Economic and Financial Indicators," December 18, 2004, p. 194.

[22] Li Ong, "Burgernomics: The Economics of the Big Mac Standard," *Journal of International Money and Finance,* vol. 16, no. 6 (December 1997), p. 865.

[23] U.S. and Chinese data on their bilateral trade differ substantially, due mainly to how each side counts Chinese exports and imports that are transshipped through Hong Kong. China counts most of its exports that go to Hong Kong but are later re-exported to the United States as Chinese exports to Hong Kong. As a result, China statistics state that it

had a $80.3 billion trade surplus with the United States in 2004. The United States counts imports from Hong Kong that originated from China as imports from China, but it often fails to attribute exports to China that pass through Hong Kong as exports to China. As a result, the United States and China cannot agree on the actual size of the U.S.-China trade imbalance. See Robert Feenstra et al., "The U.S.-China Bilateral Trade Balance: Its Size and Determinants," NBER Working Paper 6598 (June 1998).

[24] The returns to capital of U.S. owned firms in China flow to Americans.

[25] About 43% of FDI in China (based on data for 1979 to 2004) has come from Hong Kong. The United States is the second largest investor in China (at 8.5% of total FDI) followed by Japan (8.3) and Taiwan (7.0%). See CRS Issue Brief IB91121, *China's Economic Conditions*, by Wayne M. Morrison.

[26] According to Chinese data, China's largest trading deficits in 2003 were with Taiwan ($31.5 billion), South Korea ($13.1 billion), and Japan ($5.0 billion).

[27] One analyst has estimated that the domestic value-added content of Chinese exports to the United States by foreign-invested firms in China to be about 20%, while 80% comes from the value of imported parts that come into China for assembly. As a result, an appreciation of China's currency would likely have only a minor effect on China's exports to the United States (since the cost of imported inputs would fall as a result). See Testimony of Professor Lawrence J. Lau before the Congressional-Executive Commission on China, *Is China Playing by the Rules? Free Trade, Fair Trade, and WTO Compliance,* hearing, September 24, 2003.

[28] Chinese data indicate that the share of China's exports produced by foreign-invested enterprises (FIEs) in China rose from 1.9% in 1986 to 54.8% in 2003.

[29] In 2000, 2.1% of total U.S. exports went to China; this share increased to 4.2% in 2004.

[30] However, obtaining full compliance with China's WTO commitments to date has been a problem for the United States. See CRS Issue Brief IB91121, *China-U.S. Trade Issues*, by Wayne M. Morrison.

[31] Putting exchange rate issues aside, most economists maintain that trade is a win-win situation for the economy as a whole, but produces losers within the economy. This view derives from the principle of comparative advantage, which states that trade shifts production to the

goods a country is relatively talented at producing from goods it is relatively less talented at producing. As trade expands, production of goods with a comparative disadvantage will decline in the United States, to the detriment of workers and investors in those sectors (offset by higher employment and profits in sectors with a comparative advantage). Economists generally argue that free trade should be pursued because the gains from trade are large enough that the losers from trade can be compensated by the winners, and the winners will still be better off. Critics argue that the losses from free trade are not acceptable as long as the political system fails to compensate the losers fairly. See CRS Report RL32059, *Trade, Trade Barriers, and Trade Deficits: Implications for U.S. Welfare,* by Craig Elwell.

[32] On the other hand, over the long run, the fixed exchange rate encourages trade (and investment) between the two countries by eliminating exchange rate risk. In the long run, the reduced risk could make both imports and exports higher than under a floating system.

[33] Testimony of Franklin J. Vargo, National Association of Manufacturers, before the House Committee on Financial Services, Subcommittee on Domestic and International Monetary, Trade, and Technology Policy hearing, *China's Exchange Rate Regime and Its Effects on the U.S. Economy,* Oct. 1, 2003.

[34] Some commentators have compared the undervalued exchange rate to a Chinese tariff on U.S. imports. One major difference between a tariff and the peg is that a tariff does not result in any benefit to U.S. consumers, as the peg does. A more appropriate comparison might be an export subsidy, which benefits consumers who purchase the subsidized product at a lower cost, but may harm some domestic firms that must compete against the subsidized product.

[35] See CRS Report RL32350, *Deindustrialization of the U.S. Economy,* by Craig Elwell. A thorough analysis of the trend can also be found in Robert Rowthorn and Ramana Rasmaswamy, *Deindustrialization: Its Causes and Implications,* Economic Issues 10 (Washington, DC: International Monetary Fund, 1997).

[36] Council of Economic Advisers, *2003 Economic Report of the President.*

[37] Since June 2000, manufacturing output has fallen by 6% (according to the Industrial Production Index) while manufacturing employment has fallen by 15.7%. Thus, productivity has increased such that fewer workers are needed to produce a given amount of output.

[38] Lower wages alone do not give China a price advantage relative to the United States. U.S. workers are much more productive than Chinese workers, and this primarily accounts for their higher wages. Lower unit labor costs (wages divided by productivity) determine which country has a price advantage. In labor-intensive industries, China is likely to have lower unit labor costs; in knowledge-intensive industries, the United States is likely to have lower unit labor costs.

[39] Alliance Capital, Management L.P., Alliance Bernstein, U.S. Weekly Economic Update, *Manufacturing Payrolls Declining Globally: The Untold Story*, by Joseph Carson, October 10, 2003. Note that the study attributes most of the job reductions in China in the manufacturing sector to increased productivity in China. However, it is likely that the Chinese government's restructuring of inefficient state-owned enterprises, and consequent large-scale layoffs by such firms, was also a major factor.

[40] Alliance Capital, Management L.P., Alliance Bernstein, U.S. Weekly Economic Update, *Manufacturing Jobs Still Declining in Industrialized Economies*, by Joseph Carson, February 18, 2005.

[41] Federal Reserve Bank of Chicago, *Chicago Fed Letter*, November 2003.

[42] According to the study, U.S. manufactured domestic exports declined by 7.5% in 2001 and by 5.6% in 2002.

[43] See Congressional Budget Office, *Causes and Consequences of the Trade Deficit*, March 2000.

[44] Nations that fail to save enough to meet their investment needs must obtain savings from other countries with high savings rates. By obtaining resources from foreign investors for its investment needs, the United States is able to enjoy a higher rate of consumption than it would if investment were funded by domestic savings alone (although many analysts warn that America's low savings rate could be risky to the U.S. economy in the long run). The inflow of foreign capital to the United States is equivalent to the United States borrowing from the rest of the world. The only way the United States can borrow from the rest of the world is by importing more than it exports (running a trade deficit).

[45] From a political perspective, some U.S. policymakers have expressed concern over the high level of U.S. government debt owed to the Chinese government.

[46] For more information, see CRS Report RL30534, *America's Growing Current Account Deficit: Its Cause and What It Means for the Economy*, by Marc Labonte and Gail Makinen.

[47] As the above discussion implies, appreciating the yuan would likely entail costs and benefits for the U.S. economy.

[48] A middle-of- the road proposal has been made by Morris Goldstein and Nicholas Lardy, (Institute for International Economics) which would reform China's peg in two stages. During the first stage, the yuan would be appreciated by 15-25%, the currency band expanded to between five and seven percent, and the yuan would be pegged to a basket of major foreign currencies (the dollar, the yen, and the euro). In the second stage, China would, once it reformed its financial sector, adopt a managed floating exchange system. See "Two-Stage Currency Reform for China," *Wall Street Journal,* Sept. 12, 2003.

[49] Some economists argue that short-term movements in floating exchange rates cannot always be explained by economic fundamentals. If this were the case, then the floating exchange rate could become inexplicably overvalued (undervalued) at times, reducing (increasing) the output of U.S. exporters and U.S. firms that compete with Chinese imports. These economists often favor fixed or managed exchange rates to prevent these unexplainable fluctuations, which they argue are detrimental to U.S. economic well-being. Other economists argue that movements in floating exchange rates are rational, and therefore lead to economically efficient outcomes.

[50] This argument is made in Morris Goldstein and Nicholas Lardy, "A Modest Proposal for China's Renminbi,"*Financial Times*, Aug. 26, 2003. Alternatively, if Chinese citizens proved unconcerned about keeping their wealth in Chinese assets, the removal of capital controls could lead to a greater inflow of foreign capital since foreigners would be less concerned about being unable to access their Chinese investments. This would cause the exchange rate to appreciate.

[51] Another problem for China if the yuan appreciated, whether through floating or a revaluation, is that it would reduce the value of their U.S. assets. Since China held $194.5 billion of U.S. Treasury securities at the end of 2004 and $88 billion of U.S. agency debt in June 2003 — much of it in the central bank — these capital losses could potentially be very large. Unlike a private bank, a central bank does not have to worry about insolvency as a result of capital losses since they control their liabilities, but it could potentially have negative fiscal or

inflationary ramifications. See "A License to Lose Money," *The Economist*, April 30, 2005, p. 74.

[52] On October 30, 2003, the Treasury Department released its semi-annual report on foreign exchange rate policies. Although Treasury was under pressure from several Members of Congress to state that China "manipulated" its currency (which, by U.S. law, would have required Treasury to negotiate with China to end such practices), it did not make such a designation. Thus, it is unclear how hard the Bush Administration is willing to push China on this issue.

[53] Some analysts argue that China's currency peg has induced other East Asian economies, particularly Japan, Taiwan, and South Korea to intervene in currency markets to keep their currencies weak (in order to compete with Chinese exports). Thus, the United States could seek to reach a broad consensus with all the major economies in East Asia to halt or limit currency interventions.

[54] Section 301 to 309 of the 1974 Trade Act, as amended. For additional information, see CRS Report 98-454, *Section 301 of the Trade Act of 1974, as Amended: Its Operation and Issues Involving Its Use by the United States,* by Wayne Morrison.

[55] For example, the language in H.R. 3269 states that the peg violates Article XV of the General Agreement on Tariffs and Trade (GATT) agreement dealing with exchange arrangements and the WTO Agreements on Subsidies and Countervailing Measures. Other critics charge the peg violates Article XXIII of the GATT dealing with nullification or impairment of the benefits of a trade agreement.

[56] Dispute resolution in the WTO is carried out under the Dispute Resolution Understanding (DSU). See CRS Report RS20088, *Dispute Settlement in the World Trade Organization,* by Jeanne J. Grimmett.

[57] Many trade analysts argue that countries are more likely to comply with rulings by multilateral organizations to which they are parties (and whose rules they have agreed to comply with) than accede to the wishes of another country under the threat of unilateral sanctions.

[58] USTR press release, November 12, 2004.

[59] See CRS Report RS20570, *Trade Remedies and the U.S.-China Bilateral WTO Accession Agreement,* by William H. Cooper.

[60] The U.S. International Trade Commission is in charge of making market disruption determinations under the safeguard provisions for most products (with the exception of textiles and apparel, which are handled by the Committee for the Implementation of the Textile Agreements, an inter-agency committee chaired by the U.S.

Commerce Department). Import relief is subject to presidential approval. The Bush Administration has invoked the special China safeguard provisions on certain textile and apparel products.

[61] There is also the danger that if China made changes to its peg (such as appreciating the yuan to the dollar) in order to ease political pressure from the United States, it would expect something in return, such as easing U.S. pressure on China on other trade issues.

[62] International Intellectual Property Alliance, *Country Reports, China*, 2003.

[63] The Chinese government attempted to use tax rebates on value-added taxes (VAT) to assist certain domestic industries during the 1997-1998 Asian financial crisis and during the outbreak of Severe Acute Respiratory Syndrome (SARS) in 2003.

[64] *Inside U.S. Trade*, October 22, 2003.

[65] *China Daily*, October 15, 2003.

[66] This move appears to be motivated in part by a desire on the part of the Chinese government to reduce U.S. pressure on China's currency and to lessen the financial drain the rebates have on the central government's budget.

[67] China's banking system is largely controlled by the central government. Banks are directed by the government to extend loans to SOEs to help keep them financially afloat. However, in many cases, SOEs fail to repay the loans. Thus, many analysts view this system as a direct government subsidy.

[68] Even in cases where jobs have shifted from the United States and China, there are still questions as to the net impact to the United States. If the United States is no longer internationally competitive in certain industries, it may be better to shed those industries and to focus more on economic activities where the United States has a greater comparative advantage. The challenge for policymakers is how to help displaced workers get the training they need to find well-paying jobs that are comparable to or better than the jobs they lost.

[69] The World Bank, *China: Promoting Growth with Equity*, October 13, 2003, p. 9.

[70] Political arguments have been made that an economically developed China would become more peaceful and democratic. Others argue that an economically stronger China would be a more dangerous China to U.S. strategic interests.

[71] A decline in the U.S. terms of trade would mean that prices for U.S. exports would decline vis-à-vis import prices. Thus, it would take

more U.S. exports to obtain a comparable level of imports. A decline in the term of trade implies a relative (but not absolute) loss in national welfare.

[72] See World Economic Forum, *Global Competitiveness Report, 2003-2004*, October 2003.

Chapter 3

CHINA'S CURRENCY: U.S. OPTIONS[*]

Jonathan E. Sanford

SUMMARY

In recent years, the United States and other countries have expressed, with considerable concern, the view that China's national currency (the yuan or renminbi) was seriously undervalued. Some analysts say the yuan needs to rise by as much as 40% in order to reflect its true value. Critics say that, by undervaluing its currency, China gains unfair trade advantage and has seriously injured the manufacturing sector in the United States. Chinese officials say that they have not pegged the yuan to the dollar in order to gain trade advantages. Rather, they say the fixed rate promotes economic stability. Without this, they say, fluctuations in the yuan's value could cause serious dislocations in China's domestic economy.

On July 21, 2005, China announced a new foreign exchange system which is intended, officials said, to allow more flexibility and to permit the international value of the yuan to be established by market forces. The yuan was increased in value by 2% and a "crawling peg" was introduced so that the yuan could rise gradually in value. On July 27, however, Chinese officials said that they did not intend the new mechanism to produce further increases in the yuan's valuation.

---

[*] Excerpted from CRS Report RL33018, dated July 29, 2005.-3.

Together, the two announcements have sown much confusion as to China's real intent.

The Treasury Department has urged China strongly in recent years to adopt procedures that would allow the yuan to rise in value. Congress is considering legislation that would place a 27.5% tariff on Chinese imports to the United States if the yuan is not revalued. It is not clear whether the new system Chinese officials adopted will meet U.S. expectations. A Senate vote on the legislation to impose special tariffs is scheduled for late September 2005.

The United States has pursued the yuan-dollar exchange rate issue as a bilateral U.S.-China issue. Other countries are also affected by the presumably undervalued yuan — some more than the U.S. — but they have allowed the United States to take the lead. In this, they stand to benefit from any changes the U.S. effects in its confrontation with China while they take none of the blame. There are at least five ways the United States could deal with the yuan exchange rate issue. Some of these would involve other countries more explicitly in the process.

First, the United States might continue pressing China publicly for further changes in its foreign exchange system in order that the yuan's value would better reflect market conditions and economic realities. Second, the U.S. could restrict imports from China pending action to revalue the yuan. Third, the U.S. might stop pressing China publicly, on the expectation that China will move more rapidly towards reform if it is not pressured. Fourth, the U.S. might ask the IMF to determine whether China has been manipulating its currency in violation of IMF rules and whether its new exchange rate mechanism complies. Fifth, the United States might refer the issue to the World Trade Organization (WTO), asserting that the United States has been injured by unfair trade practices linked to the undervaluation of China's currency and asking the WTO to authorize trade remedies (tariffs on Chinese goods, for example) aimed at correcting this abuse. This report will be updated as new developments arise.

SCOPE AND PURPOSE OF THIS CHAPTER

In recent years, the United States and China have disagreed whether China's national currency, the yuan or renminbi, is properly valued compared to the U.S. dollar and whether China is manipulating its currency.[1] The United States has pushed China to raise the value of its currency. Chinese officials say they want to make their exchange rate system more flexible, but China also needs long-term stability in its currency value in order to avoid dislocations. Chinese officials also say they will not bow to foreign pressure. China announced a new exchange rate procedure on July 21, 2005. This report summarizes this controversy, it describes actions and positions taken by the United States, China and other countries, and it discusses various approaches the United States might use to address this concern.

The IMF says, in Article IV of its Articles of Agreement that countries shall "Avoid manipulating exchange rates or the international monetary system in order to prevent effective balance of payments adjustment or to gain an unfair competitive advantage over other members."[2] The U.S. Omnibus Trade and Competitiveness of 1988 requires (sec. 3004) that the Secretary of the Treasury determine whether other countries "manipulate the rate of exchange between their currency and the United States dollar for the purpose of preventing effective balance of payments adjustments or gaining unfair competitive advantage in international trade.[3]

YUAN-DOLLAR EXCHANGE RATE ISSUE

Is China's Currency Undervalued?

From 1994 until recently, China's central bank pegged the yuan at roughly 8.3 to the dollar, and it held the yuan at that value by buying or selling dollars or dollar-based assets in the market. Under a floating exchange rate system, by contrast, the yuan's value would be determined by the relative supply and demand for goods and services in the two countries and the relative demand for each currency in the market.

Critics claim that China's currency is significantly undervalued vis-a-vis the U.S. dollar (perhaps by as much as 40%) and that this hinders U.S. exports to China and gives Chinese firms a price advantage in their exports to the United States and other countries. They say that China's currency is held by government action at a level well below its true level and that, without official manipulation, the value of the yuan would rise substantially. Critics say that China's undervalued currency has added to the U.S. trade deficit and hurt output and employment in the manufacturing sectors of the U.S. economy. Many have urged the Administration to put pressure on Chinese officials in order to stop them from manipulating the yuan. They say

China should either raise the international value of the yuan by official action ("revalue") or let the yuan trade freely in foreign exchange markets ("float") so that the free market can determine its international value.

Chinese officials have argued that the fixed exchange rate between their currency and the U.S. dollar is not intended to promote exports but rather to promote economic stability. They worry that an economic crisis could ensue in China, with serious negative effects on employment, growth and their economic reform program, if the dollar-yuan exchange rate were to fluctuate widely. In particular, they worry that their weak domestic banking system might be unable to cope with any speculative pressure that might follow the advent of a more flexible exchange rate system and more open capital markets. Chinese officials say the Asian financial crisis of 1997-1998 was caused mainly by the combined effect of convertible currencies and poorly regulated financial systems. Pegging their exchange rate will help them avoid the dangers, they claim, which precipitated the Asian crisis.

Partly as a result of currency values and partly as a result of the need by the United States to borrow foreign funds to finance its Federal budget and its foreign trade deficits, China has accumulated large reserves of U.S. dollars and U.S. dollar-denominated assets. China's foreign reserves have grown rapidly in the past decade and now total more than $711 billion. Accumulating foreign reserves in this manner puts substantial pressure on China's internal financial system. To offset possible inflationary pressure, China has had to restrict monetary growth and to regulate capital inflows. Over the long term, such actions may cause dislocations in China's domestic economy. However, if the yuan is at an advantageous exchange rate, China's export prospects are enhanced and foreign investment in its economy is encouraged. So long as China is willing to continue accumulating foreign exchange and to accept its domestic consequences, the Chinese authorities should be able to hold down the international value of the yuan for a considerable period of time.

China announced a new exchange rate mechanism on July 21, 2005.[4] Many believe the new system will rectify the situation. Others are concerned, however, that the new procedures will be only fitfully employed and China will continue to manipulate and undervalue its currency.

Currency Manipulation

Many Exchange Rate Systems

The issue of currency manipulation is difficult and complex. Until the early 1970s, the IMF played the central role in world exchange rates. All currencies had a fixed value compared to the U.S. dollar and the U.S. dollar had a fixed value compared to gold. If countries wanted to change their par value compared to the U.S. dollar, the IMF had to first approve. Since 1976, however, with passage of the Second Amendment to the IMF Articles of Agreement, each country is free to determine the exchange rate system it will use. Some countries have floated the value of their currency in world money markets, others have fixed the value of their currency to that of another major country, and others have pursued a mixed strategy.

IMF Surveillance

The IMF is responsible for surveillance, under Article IV of its charter, to ensure that countries comply with basic standards. Article IV prohibits countries from manipulating their exchange rates in order to gain unfair trade advantage. It also says that "the Fund shall exercise firm surveillance over the exchange rate policies of members, and shall adopt specific principles for the guidance of all members with respect to those policies." Its current principles for surveillance were adopted by the IMF executive board in 1979 and have been revised periodically since.[5]

The principles say, in effect, that countries may peg the value of their currency to another currency but they cannot do this in ways which violate the requirements of Article IV. Basically, the pegged rate needs to reflect a country's underlying economic realities. These include, for example, changes in the volume and composition of its domestic output, in the size, composition and direction of its foreign trade, in its domestic rates of growth and national income, in the size of its reserves and in shifts in its domestic fiscal and monetary policies. Countries may hold the value of their currencies at a fixed rate under this system for a long period of time. Whether this is manipulation in violation of Article IV depends on the economic conditions and the way a country holds the value of its currency constant.[6]

Manipulation Defined

Persistent intervention in exchange rate markets is one indicator for manipulation. According to the IMF principles for surveillance, countries may intervene in foreign exchange markets to counter short-term disorderly conditions that cause disruptive short-term movements in the exchange value of their currencies. However, the IMF guidelines say that other kinds of intervention "might indicate the need for discussion with a member." These include "protracted large-scale intervention in one direction in the exchange market" and "behavior of the exchange rate that appears to be unrelated to underlying economic and financial conditions including factors affecting competitiveness and long-term capital movements." As may be seen below, China's management of its foreign exchange system has given rise to concern that it has been or may be violating these criteria.

Countries are allowed, under the guidelines, to use their exchange rates to promote growth and development. The IMF rules for surveillance say the Fund's appraisal of country policies "shall take into account the extent to which the policies of a member, including its exchange rate policies, serve the objectives of the continuing development of orderly underlying conditions that are necessary for financial stability, the promotion of sustainable economic growth, and reasonable levels of employment." However, countries are also required to "take into account in their intervention policies the interests of other members, including those of the countries in whose currencies they intervene." In other words, countries can use exchange rate policy to help sustain growth and employment in their domestic economy but they cannot use an unrealistic exchange rate to prevent balance of payments (BOP) adjustment or to gain unfair trade advantages. Adjustment includes such things as increased imports, capital inflows to fund BOP deficits or outflows to offset BOP surpluses, increased domestic interest rates or price levels, the accumulation of excess reserves, etc. If one country does not adjust its BOP imbalance, the burden of adjustment will be thrown upon its trading partners through monetary contraction, unemployment and the like.

China and Manipulation

China says that it needs exchange rate stability to avoid injury to its domestic economy. The issue is whether China's old and new procedures for attaining stability are throwing undue burdens onto other countries and violating the prohibition against manipulation.

Most countries which seek to sustain unrealistic exchange rates for their currencies eventually find, as did several major Asian countries during the foreign exchange and BOP crisis of the late 1990s, that their foreign exchange reserves are insufficient to maintain their currency at the desired value indefinitely. In most cases, countries have tried to value their currency at a higher level than the market might otherwise find appropriate. This raises the income level for their people and it lowers the price of imports. If confidence in the government's economic management disappears, people holding their national currency will increasingly desire to exchange it for established foreign currencies such as the dollar. When the government runs out of dollars and other such foreign exchange, it can no longer "defend" its currency and devaluation follows.

In the case of China, however, critics argue that the yuan has been kept at an international value lower than its actual market value. This increases exports but it raises the cost of imports and lowers domestic income. However, this also stimulates domestic economic growth and employment, though at some risk that too much stimulation might cause the economy to overheat. Other domestic economic policies need to be oriented to keep this stimulus under control.

As long as the Chinese authorities are willing to sell yuan and buy foreign currency, they can keep their currency from rising in value compared to other countries. China has $711 billion in foreign exchange reserves. If it is willing to accumulate further reserves, with the attendant risk of inflation and other forms of financial dislocation, China may hold the exchange value of its currency below its real international value for a long time.

Some would argue that an ability to maintain one's currency at a fixed level through market interventions, without regard for underlying economic conditions, is evidence of manipulation. Others would argue, however, that the economic benefits of stability are important and are shared by many countries. Moreover, they might contend, efforts to influence exchange rates through intervention in currency markets are not much different in their effect than are the changes in interest rates and other policies that countries with floating exchange rates use to influence the exchange rate of their currencies.

The New System Announced July 21

The New Exchange Rate Mechanism

On July 21, 2005, the People's Bank of China (PBC), the central bank for mainland China,[7] announced that — rather than being pegged only against the dollar — the value of the yuan would be pegged in the future against a basket of currencies. The composition of the basket would not be disclosed. The central bank also announced that the yuan would be revalued (increased in value) against the dollar by 2.1% (to 8.11 yuan per dollar) and its daily value compared to the new basket of currencies would be allowed to vary by 0.3% each day above or below a central parity. The PBC said that "the closing price of a foreign currency such as the US dollar traded against the RMB [yuan]...after the closing of the market each working day" will become "the central parity for the trading against the RMB the following working day."[8] Economists call this kind of exchange rate mechanism a "crawling peg" because it allows currency values to be adjusted in small increments over a period of time either in response to market forces or to official announcements.

On July 27, 2005, however, the People's Bank of China (PBC) announced that no further increases in the international value of the yuan were to be expected. It said, as regards the July 21 announcement, that "This certainly does not mean that the 2 per cent adjustment of the renminbi is the first step that will be followed by gf8further adjustment."[9] The central bank blamed the press for "creating misunderstanding"and creating expectations that the procedures introduced on July 21 would result in further increases in the value of the yuan. Four days earlier, on July 23, the governor of China's central bank had fueled expectations that the yuan would rise in value. Explaining the new exchange rate mechanism on national television, he told viewers that "We have made an initial adjustment to the exchange rate level of 2 percent," implying that further adjustments were to come.[10]

Interpreting the Two Announcements

The July 27 announcement can be interpreted two ways. First, it can be seen as a statement that China does not really intend to allow the yuan to increase in value, as the procedures announced July 21 would suggest. If this is true, the new crawling peg mechanism would not be allowed to function and China's currency would stay at about its current level. This might satisfy internal critics who dislike the plan to increase the value of the yuan. On the other hand, if the new announcement reflects China's actual policy, it makes little sense for Chinese authorities to make that statement (as they did) just before the U.S. Congress was scheduled to consider legislation affecting China and the IMF was scheduled to discuss whether China is in compliance with its exchange rate obligations.

Alternatively, the new announcement can be seen as a tactical move to discourage speculators. In order to prevent its accumulation of foreign exchange assets from destabilizing China's internal financial system, the government has had to institute a strict system of capital import controls. Analysts worry that massive speculative inflows might overwhelm these controls and seriously destabilize China's economy. They would also make it more difficult for the central bank to implement a crawling peg mechanism which seeks gradual but continued increases in the value of the yuan. Many analysts worry that, if the yuan is going to increase in value considerably on account of the new procedures announced July 21, currency speculators have every reason to buy yuan and yuan-denominated assets as soon as possible. Doing so, they guarantee themselves large profits (when they convert their yuan back into foreign exchange) as the yuan increases in value. This would be a one-way bet that speculators could not lose, since there was little chance the yuan would fall in value.[11]

From this second point of view, the central bank's announcement on July 27 is not evidence that Chinese officials are shying away from their plan to revalue the yuan. Rather, it is evidence that they intend to do so even though they must walk a narrow and precarious path — discouraging speculators at the same time that they do what the speculators expect — to accomplish that end. Whether China will be able to proceed with its plans for a long-term upward adjustment in the yuan remains to be seen. Too much speculative pressure, too many people seeking to buy yuan, could force China to accelerate the adjustment process in order to limit the destabilizing effects that such speculation might have on the Chinese economy.

U.S. officials seem to have adopted the second interpretation of the July 27 announcement. A Treasury Department spokesman said that China's reform mechanism will allow greater flexibility in the yuan exchange rate over time.[12] Meanwhile, Senator Schumer also said, noting the new announcement, that "we trust that the Chinese will allow market forces to work." He also said that he and others would carefully monitor the process during the next few months.[13]

On July 28, however, Senators Schumer and Graham announced that they were not satisfied with China's progress in reforming its foreign exchange procedures and they might press for action on their tariff legislation (see below) around October 1. They seem to have concluded that the July 27 statement better reflects China's real position. "I can tell you that we are not satisfied with simply a 2 % revaluation," Senator Schumer said. "We don't want to tell the Chinese how to do it and we understand that it will take some time." Some analysts have speculated that, given their two recent announcements, Chinese officials want to drag the adjustment process out — at perhaps 2% a year — for as long as possible.[14]

Issues about Implementation

It is not evident that the new system announced July 21 will satisfy many of the concerns previously raised against China's old exchange rate system. Likewise, it is possible — even if the yuan goes up in value compared to the U.S. dollar — that the new system may have both desirable and undesirable consequences for the United States.

First, the yuan will increase in value in the new system only if the central bank allows the daily changes to be cumulative. If this happens, the yuan could increase in value by as much as 1.5% each week or as much as 30% in five months. In the old system, "daily changes in the value of the renminbi against the U.S. dollar [were] limited to 0.3% on either side of the basic rate" established by the central bank.[15] The central bank bought or sold currency to return this "market" rate to its official level each day. The central bank will also need to trade currencies under the new system to keep changes in the yuan's value from exceeding the 0.3% daily limit. In the process, if the July 27 statement reflects its actual position, it could buy or sell additional currency in order to keep the yuan's "market" rate at any level it believes appropriate. No announcement would be necessary and it would be difficult to prove whether this was taking place. China could always claim that the current exchange rate was set by the market and not by official policy. The Chinese government has not announced any procedures or guidelines for the central bank's daily interventions in currency markets in the new system put into effect July 21.

Second, it is not evident, that the value of the yuan in the new system would respond to changes in China's economic relations with other countries. The dollar might go down in value compared to the yuan in certain circumstances, for instance, but this change would be limited by the offsetting changes in the value of the other currencies in the central bank's currency basket. The yuan will still be fixed in value compared to this basket of currencies. It is conceivable, for example, that the prevailing trends in China's economic relationship with the United States would suggest a need for the dollar to go down in value compared to the yuan. However, if the dollar went up in value compared to the euro or other currencies in China's currency basket, the dollar would have to go up compared to the yuan in order to offset the falling value of those currencies. Thus, the dollar price of China's exports might depend more on changes in the relative value of the currencies in the central bank's currency basket than it would on China's actual economic situation.

Third, under the new system, China will not need to hold or acquire as many dollars as before in order to stabilize the price of its currency. To stabilize the value of the yuan compared to the currency basket, it may need to buy euros or yen or some other currency instead. If China is accumulating fewer dollars than before, it will have less need to purchase dollar-denominated securities. If China's future purchases in U.S. securities markets declines, the sellers of dollar-denominated notes and bonds may find that they need to offer higher interest rates than before in order to attract new buyers for the securities previously bought by China. The result would likely be an increase in market interest rates in the United States.

U.S. Treasury Actions

The Omnibus Trade and Competitiveness Act of 1988 (sec. 3004) requires the Secretary of the Treasury to determine, in consultation with the International Monetary Fund, whether countries are manipulating the value of their currency in order to gain unfair trade advantage. If the Secretary finds there is manipulation, he or she must "initiate negotiations with such foreign countries on an expedited basis, in the International Monetary Fund or bilaterally, for the purpose of ensuring that countries promptly address the rate of exchange between their currencies and the United States dollar" in order to permit effective balance of payments adjustment and to eliminate any unfair trade advantages they might have gained from manipulation.[16] The Secretary is required (sec. 3005) to report to Congress twice annually on the international economic and exchange rate policies of other countries.

U.S. officials have spoken with Chinese officials and issued statements on several occasions, urging China to reform its exchange rate system so it would be more flexible or to let it operate according to market principles. There is no indication on the public record, though, as to whether — as required by the 1988 trade law — U.S. officials have consulted with the IMF on this matter or what, if any, response the IMF has made. In May 2005, the Treasury Department reported, in a sec. 3005 report to Congress, that China was not manipulating its exchange rate in violation of its obligations under Article IV of the IMF charter.[17] As noted above, the language of Article IV and the language of the relevant U.S. law are essentially the same.

The Treasury Department's conclusions in its 2005 report rely more on statements that China is laying the groundwork for a future revaluation of its currency than on they do on any determination that China's prevailing exchange rate policies were appropriate. Some observers suggest, though, that the Treasury Department was more critical of China in this report than it was previously in part due to congressional pressure. The report said that, "If current trends continue without substantial alteration [i.e., revaluation], China's policies will likely meet the statute's technical requirements" for designating China as a country which unfairly manipulates its currency value. Treasury Secretary John Snow reportedly gave Chinese officials six months to rectify the situation. Treasury officials later said, however, that China should revalue its currency immediately by 10% against the dollar or risk contrary legislation from Congress.[18]

On July 21, 2005, in his official response to China's new exchange rate system, Secretary Snow said that he welcomed the announcement that China is adopting a more flexible exchange rate regime in which the value of its currency would be based on market supply. He noted, however, that "We will monitor China's managed float as their exchange rate moves to alignment with underlying market conditions."[19] Interviewed that evening on the PBS *Nightly Business Review*, he said he was encouraged that China had "put in place a mechanism to allow their currency to better reflect market conditions, demand and supply conditions, and to move in accordance with the marketplace." He agreed that the initial 2% change was small, but he said the important thing was the commitment they have expressed to flexibility. "The really important thing that's happened today is the long term," he said. "This is the start of a process and the Chinese have indicated they want to get their currency based on markets rather than a peg."[20]

Congressional Initiatives

Meanwhile, Congress is considering legislation that would limit China's access to the U.S. market if it does not stop manipulating the value of its currency. On April 6, 2005, for example, Senators Charles Schumer and Lindsey Graham proposed that Congress enact a 27.5% tariff on all Chinese products entering the United States if China does not raise the value of its currency.[21] The Senate voted 67-33 to endorse this proposal and a final vote on the measure was planed to occur on or before July 27, 2005. On June 30, 2005, Treasury Secretary Snow and Federal Reserve Chairman Greenspan assured Senators Schumer, Graham and others that China is moving to revise its exchange rate policies. On the basis of those assurances, the Senators agreed to postponed until September any vote on their bill requiring tariff sanctions on Chinese imports if China does not revalue the yuan.[22] Senator Schumer was quoted as saying, after Chinese officials announced the 2% revaluation of the yuan and adoption of a new exchange rate system, that "It is smaller than we had hoped, but to paraphrase the Chinese philosophers, a trip of a thousand miles can begin with the first baby step."[23]

On July 27, 2005, the House of Representatives passed legislation (H.R. 3283) proposed by Representative Phil English which addressed the Chinese exchange rate issues in several ways. First, the legislation would make imports from non-market economies (such as China) subject to the U.S. laws that authorize the imposition of special tariffs (countervailing duties) against foreign goods which cause injury to U.S. producers if those goods are found to have benefitted from subsidies from foreign governments. It also tightens the rules on anti-dumping duties to prevent nonpayment of penalties by those found in violation of those U.S. laws. Countervailing duties and anti-dumping provisions are allowed under the rules of the World Trade Organization (WTO). The bill establishes a comprehensive monitoring system to track China's compliance with specific WTO commitments and it requires periodic reports on China's progress on meeting those commitments. It also requires the Treasury Department to define the term "currency manipulation" for the purposes of U.S. law and it requires the Department to report periodically on China's implementation of its new currency regime. The bill passed (255 to 168) on July 27, 2005. Senator Susan Collins has introduced a similar bill (S. 1421) in the Senate.

Congress is also considering other legislation on to this issue. On April 7, 2005, for example, Representatives Duncan Hunter and Tim Ryan introduced legislation that would make it easier for U.S. firms to file complaints with the World Trade Organization (WTO) claiming that currency manipulation is a trade-distorting practice.[24]

The new Chinese exchange rate procedure was announced less than a week before Congress was originally scheduled to consider the Schumer/Graham legislation and the English bill. Though most observers welcome the change in the Chinese procedure, many question whether the new procedure will achieve a significant change in the yuan's value vis-a-vis the dollar and whether Chinese officials will foreswear manipulation. Some observers also suggest that the new system was intended to be a means for deflecting criticism, for weakening the pressure for change, and for preventing or delaying passage of strong legislation.[25]

Other Countries' Views

No other country has taken as strong a position on the Chinese exchange rate issue as has the United States. Bank of Canada Governor David Dodge called on China in early June 2005 to free its currency from the fixed rate against the U.S. dollar or to risk sparking U.S. and European trade protectionism. He did not propose that sanctions or economic pressure should be adopted, however, in order to help encourage China towards that end.[26]

Other countries have reportedly been strong, in their private discussions with China, in urging a rapid resolution of the exchange rate issue. In their public comments, however, most have taken a softer line. In June 2005, Japan's finance minister urged China to reform its tight currency peg on grounds that the current yuan-dollar exchange rate was hurting the Chinese economy and causing it to overheat.[27] The same month, after Chinese Premier Wen Jiabao told an Asia-Europe ministerial meeting that China would adopt a more flexible currency policy only when it believed itself ready, European ministers said that they hoped it would not take too long[28] but they agreed that China should not be pressured and it had the right to determine when and how it would reform its currency.[29]

Though the issue was discussed at their 2005 summit meeting in Scotland, the Group of Eight major industrial countries (G8) did not to mention the yuan exchange rate issue in their final communique. China's President told the G8 at this meeting that China wanted to base the yuan's value on market forces but it would do this on its own time and not as a result of foreign pressure.[30] Some analysts suggest that the G8's public silence on the yuan question was calculated to provide China with a "narrow window of opportunity" allowing China to "inch towards a more flexible exchange rate policy without losing face by appearing to bow to foreign pressure.[32]

OPTIONS FOR THE UNITED STATES

There are several approaches the United States might use for encouraging China to implement the July 21 crawling peg procedure it previously announced or to improve on it. These options or policy tools are not mutually exclusive, though it might be difficult for the United States to pursue some of them simultaneously. First, the U.S. Government might continue pressing China publicly for additional changes in its foreign exchange system in order to make the international value of the yuan better reflect market conditions and economic realities. Second, the United States could enact legislation restricting Chinese exports to the United States if value of the yuan is not increased. Third, the U.S. Government might stop pressing China publicly, on the expectation that China will move more rapidly towards reform if it is not pressured from abroad. Fourth, the U.S.

Government might refer the question to the IMF, asking the international agency to determine whether China has been manipulating its currency in violation of IMF rules and whether its new exchange rate mechanism complies. Fifth, the U.S. Government might refer the issue to the World Trade Organization (WTO), asserting that the United States has been injured by unfair trade practices linked to the undervaluation of China's currency and asking the WTO to authorize trade remedies (tariffs on Chinese goods, for example) aimed at correcting this abuse.

Continue Public Pressure

Continued public pressure is one method the United States might use to encourage China to adopt further reforms in its foreign exchange procedures. In particular, this might push Chinese officials to address the discrepancies between their July 21 and July 27 announcements and possible difficulties with the July 21 plan. They might be pressed, by official statements and the prospect of potential legislation, to clarify whether the "crawling peg" provisions of the July 21 plan will be allowed to work or whether China will prevent (as announced July 27) the daily changes in the value of the yuan from being cumulative. Alternatively, the United States could pressure China to adopt a different foreign exchange process that will revalue its currency more quickly.

From this perspective, it would be helpful to know whether Chinese officials intend to move towards a market-based valuation of the yuan or whether their recent announcements are designed to deflect pressure and to delay the process as much as possible. If China adopted the reforms announced to date mainly in response to foreign pressure, then it is possible that further pressure might persuade them to go further. However, if Chinese officials adopted these recent changes because they believe that market-based reform is in China's best interests, foreign pressure can either enhance or complicate their progress. China has a long tradition, in reaction to the capitulations that outsiders extracted from China in earlier centuries, of not giving in to foreign pressure. Foreign pressure might strengthen the hand of the reformers, but it might also stiffen resistence by the opponents of reform and make it harder for the reformers to achieve their ends.

It might be helpful, if the U.S. Government decides to press China for more rapid and broader reforms in their exchange rate system, if U.S. officials and legislators had more information about China's internal decision making process. How strong are the reformers? What key choices do Chinese officials believe they face as regards the economy and value of the yuan? Would the United States be pushing against a closed door if it sought faster and broader reform or is the door at least partly open? In the latter case, will the door open further or will it close and lock itself when it feels foreign pressure? This is a dilemma. Pressure might work if the Chinese authorities does not really want to reform and if their recent announcements are intended to deflect or delay criticism. Pressure might be counterproductive, on the other hand, if Chinese officials really want to reform and their recent announcements are a blueprint to the future. In the latter case, public pressure might weaken the proponents of reform and cause China to slow the process of reform.

The dilemma may be less of a concern if the United States wants to push China into adopting exchange rate reforms which exceed those which most Chinese proponents of reform will accept. This might include, for examples, efforts to accelerate the pace of the exchange rate liberalization process beyond the rate which Chinese officials believe prudent for their economy. A close examination of the Chinese policy process might show whether it is likely that foreign pressure can accomplish such goals or an alternative approach might be more effective. The latter might include, for example, efforts to persuade China that it has more economic options than it thinks and that rapid increase in the value of it currency would not produce the results that Chinese officials fear.

The other question is whether the United States would have the support of other countries if it sought to press China to adopt further reforms. It is possible that other countries might be prepared to follow the U.S. lead, now that China has announced the July 21 program of reform. In that case, they would be urging Chinese officials to proceed with a plan which has already been announced rather than pressing them to do something new. However, it is also possible that other countries will stand aside — as the Europeans, Japanese and others have done to date — in order to let the United States make this effort on its own. They would stand to benefit from any changes China might adopt but they could decide (as they seem to have done to date) that it might be more advantageous for them to show understanding towards the Chinese position in their public stance.

Restrict Exports to the United States

Alternatively, instead of using verbal pressure, the United States could adopt legislation restricting China's access to the U.S. market until it raises the value of its currency. The English bill (H.R. 3282) and the proposed Schumer/Graham amendment (both mentioned above) would have this effect. By raising the price of Chinese imports, they would reduce the flow of Chinese exports to the United States. Among other things, this would make U.S. products more competitive with Chinese goods in the United States, with some possible positive employment effects in competing U.S. industries. It would also raise the prices paid by U.S. purchasers.

It is unclear what the Chinese authorities would do if faced by restrictive import legislation of this sort. It is possible that they would raise the value of the yuan in hopes that this will eliminate the new U.S. tariffs on their goods. There being no internationally recognized standard, however, it would be uncertain how much the yuan would need to be increased in order to satisfy U.S. requirements. China could make unilateral changes in its exchange rate in hopes of finding one that satisfied U.S. concerns. Alternatively, the issue could be settled by negotiations. The yuan exchange rate being a matter which affects many countries, it seems unlikely that China and its other major trading partners would wish to see the question settled through bilateral talks with the United States alone.

Alternatively, being a member of the World Trade Organization, China might ask the WTO to examine the issue. It could ask a dispute settlement panel to rule that the United States acted in a manner inconsistent with its obligations under WTO rules when it adopted unilateral tariffs and duties aimed at China. It is uncertain, under its rules and precedents, how the WTO would respond to such a complaint. For example, countervailing duties and anti-dumping penalties are permissible under WTO rules. However, exchange rates are not normally part of that calculation. The WTO might have concern that the rules governing the world trade would be difficult to enforce if countries were free do impose countervailing duties whenever they found that foreign goods were being subsidized because they decided unilaterally that the exporting country had allowed its currency to become undervalued.

The WTO might authorize China to apply comparable restrictions of its own but the impact these might have on U.S. exports to China would likely be less than the impact the U.S. charges had on Chinese exports to the United States. Ultimately, much will likely depend on whether other countries support the U.S. or the Chinese side in this dispute. Also important would be any effects that the resulting trade dispute between the United States and China might have on the broader picture of world trade negotiations.

If the volume of Chinese exports to the United States declines because of new trade legislation, the profits of the foreign firms located in China which produce those goods will likely go down as well. Depending on technical factors, some of those firms may be able to shift production to other countries in the region. In that case, unless the currencies of those other countries should increase make their exports uncompetitive, it is possible that the issue of low-cost Chinese goods may be superceded by a similar controversy about low-cost goods from other Asian countries. It is not clear whether the legislative tools currently being considered for use against China would be applicable as well in situations of that sort.

Pursue a Policy of Restraint

Instead of pressing China publicly for reform, the United States might decide on a policy of restraint. This approach presumes that the Chinese authorities want to proceed with their reform program as rapidly as economic conditions and the prevailing policy consensus in China permit. This approach also presumes that overt pressure would be counterproductive, slowing the process and strengthening the hand of those in China who oppose reform.

It might be argued that the United States should keep its trade and currency dispute with China in perspective. The economic issues are important, one might argue, but it is also important not to raise tensions to the point where China becomes reluctant to cooperate with the United States on other issues, such as North Korea's policies on nuclear weapons. Others might respond, however, that China will cooperate with the United States in other areas when it believes that this serves its interests even though there are other areas as trade and currency policy where the two countries disagree.

Ironically, it is possible that some form of pressure may be required to move China forward on its plans for foreign exchange reform whether or not Chinese officials really want to reform. If the recent announcements were made only to distract foreign critics and to sidestep contrary action by Congress or the IMF, then a reduction in the amplitude of the pressure will be followed by a diminution in the pace of reforms. On the other hand, even if Chinese authorities want to move forward with their reform program, they may need some external pressure — if only in the form of agreed deadlines and benchmarks — to help them overcome inertia when they encounter difficult choices as they put their currency reform policies into effect.

Take It to the IMF

The United States could also pursue issue of China's exchange rate policy at the International Monetary Fund. Rather than treating it as though it were a bilateral dispute between the United States and China, the Administration could ask the IMF to determine whether China's exchange rate system is consistent with the IMF's rules or whether China needs to take additional steps in order to comply. The later might include, for instance, assurances that the crawling peg mechanism will be allowed to work or benchmarks for measuring its implementation. Among other things, the executive directors can require China to clarify whether the July 21 or the July 27 announcement reflects actual policy. China's exchange rate policies are a multilateral issue which affect other countries in addition to the United States. Most have chosen not to challenge China publicly about its foreign exchange policies. However, when the issue is laid before their representatives on the IMF's Board of Executive Directors for confidential discussion they would have to take a position and they are more likely to be frank.

The IMF staff has finished preparation of its Article IV report on China for 2005 and the executive board is reportedly scheduled to consider it August 3, 2005. Not a pro forma exercise, this is generally a substantive review and discussion by the executive directors of the major issues and policies affecting a country's economy. Exchange rate policies are a key factor in the executive board review. The board has before it the staff's written analysis but the executive directors are free to make their own analysis and to find their own conclusions. Among other things, the board will likely consider whether China's newly announced exchange rate mechanism complies with the requirements of Article IV and whether assurances are needed to insure that it will be implemented effectively.

In its 2004 Article IV review of China's economy, the IMF staff reported that it was "difficult to find persuasive evidence that the renminbi [yuan] is substantially undervalued."[32] It is likely that the IMF staff wished to avoid entanglement in a controversy which had seemingly become as much political as it was economic. Nevertheless, the staff's analysis of Chinese economic policy showed that more exchange rate flexibility, tighter monetary policy, and a reduction in the inflow of money from abroad were needed.[33] Revaluation of the yuan would be consistent with the staff's recommendations.

The IMF executive board said, in its discussion of the issue in 2004, that greater exchange rate flexibility is in China's best interest.[34] They welcomed the statement by Chinese authorities that they aimed (in the words of the IMF summary of the board discussion) "to introduce, in a phased manner, greater exchange rate flexibility," though several Directors said the timing of that change should be left to China. Many Directors also said that "it would be advantageous for China to make an initial move towards greater exchange rate flexibility without undue delay," with some preferring that this decision should be made soon. Many Directors also noted, though, that China would need to sequence the elements of this change carefully, in relation to other steps being taken to liberalize and reform capital markets, the capital account and the financial sector.

The Chinese announced their July 21 exchange rate procedures less than two weeks before the IMF executive board was scheduled to discuss their economic policies and exchange rate. They had talked, during the year following the board's meeting about them in 2004, about various possibilities but they had not taken any action. On July 21, IMF officials told the press, in response to the introduction of the new procedures, that China should not limit the renminbi's movements within the new foreign exchange framework.[35] IMF spokesman Thomas Dawson also told a press conference the same day that "We would encourage the authorities to utilize fully the scope for flexibility in the new exchange arrangement. We are ready to work with the authorities on the continuing evolution of the exchange rate system." The IMF staff does not speak for the executive board. Nevertheless, it would appear, from these indications, that the IMF views the 2.1% revaluation as the beginning, not the end, of the process for adjusting the yuan's exchange rate.

The IMF cannot make a country revise its exchange rate. Nevertheless, a statement by the IMF staff or the executive board can have significant impact on currency markets and on the policies of other countries. A statement criticizing the economic management of a country, for example, can influence the way the private sector — particularly the financial sector — deals with that country. Likewise, statements from the IMF executive board can have an affect on the policies of its member countries. If the executive board says that a country is not complying with its obligations to the IMF, countries are likely to take the IMF's position into account when they make policy on that issue.[36]

The United States does not have to wait until the IMF does its 2006 annual Article IV review in order for it to get the China exchange rate issue on the agenda of the IMF executive board once again. Rather, it need only tell the IMF Managing Director that it believes China is not complying with the requirements of Article IV.[37] The Managing Director would then be required to consult with the Chinese and to report his findings formally or informally to the executive board. A formal report would provide the United States with an occasion for asking the board to reconsider the issue again in the light of developments which have occurred since the last Article IV report. If the United States believed, for example, that China were interfering with the operations of its crawling peg mechanism in order to keep down the value of the yuan, it could ask the executive board for a finding critical of China's actions. This would be stronger, in its international impact, than a comparable finding by the Secretary of the Treasury in a semi-annual report on China's exchange rate practices.

It would be difficult for the United States to put bilateral pressure on China while the IMF is considering whether that country's exchange rate procedures comply with IMF guidelines and IMF rules. An IMF statement that China's procedures were not in compliance with the rules might help the United States marshal support from other countries if it decided to begin pressing China for action once again. On the other hand, if the executive board were to rule that China's procedures are acceptable — even though the Chinese Government was limiting the daily movements of the yuan in order to keep it from increasing much in value — the United States would have difficulty arguing the contrary view. The United States might wish to consult with the G8 countries and with other countries in order to prepare the groundwork and build a consensus before it formally brings the issue to the IMF.

Apply to the WTO

The United States could also file a complaint with the World Trade Organization (WTO) alleging that China has obtained an unfair trade advantage for its exports by keeping the value of its currency artificially low. The WTO has no authority to address exchange rate issues. However, the IMF and WTO have an agreement which requires the WTO will refer exchange rate disputes of this sort to the international monetary body and will accept the IMF's findings as conclusive.[38] By itself, a finding by the IMF that China is manipulating its currency in violation of Article IV would have no "teeth" that would require Chinese officials to change their procedures. Considered in conjunction with a trade complaint before the WTO, however, an IMF finding of this sort could result in trade sanctions if a WTO dispute reconciliation panel found that China was subsidizing its exports by undervaluing its currency.

If a WTO dispute settlement panel were to rule that China was gaining
unfair trade advantage through a low valuation of its currency, it might
authorize the United States to adopt special tariffs penalizing China if it fails
to revalue its currency. If countries join the U.S. complaint, they would also
be empowered to adopt similar tariff penalties. It might be awkward for the
United States to apply to the WTO in the manner if it has already enacted
tariff restrictions on its own. Moreover, it would be risky for the United
States to apply to the WTO for relief if it does not know beforehand how the
IMF would rule on the exchange rate issue. Support from the other major
members of the IMF would be critical for this approach to work. The G8
countries and other members of the European Union comprise a majority of
the voting power in the IMF. Consultation with these countries might be
appropriate before the United States approaches the WTO with a complaint.

RERERENCES

[1] For a comprehensive discussion of the exchange rate issue, see CRS
     Report RS21625, *China's Currency Peg: A Summary of the Economic
     Issues*, updated April 25, 2005, and CRS Report RL32165, *China's
     Exchange Rate Peg: Economic Issues and Options for U.S. Trade
     Policy*, updated May 10, 2005. See also CRS Issue Brief IB91121,
     U.S.-China Trade Issues, updated July 22, 2005. The term "renminbi"
     means "people's currency" while "yuan" is the unit of account (one
     yuan, two yuan, etc.)
[2] Articles of Agreement of the International Monetary Fund. Entered
     into force December 27, 1945. 60 Stat. 1401, TAIS 1501.
[3] The Omnibus Trade and Competitiveness Act of 1988, P.L. 100-418
     as amended.
[4] People's Bank of China. *Public Announcement of the People's Bank of
     China on Reforming th RMB Exchange Rate Regime.* July 21, 2005
     (Beijing   time.)   Available   at
     [http://www.pbc.gov.cn/english/detail.asp?col=6400&id=542].
[5] The IMF's detailed procedures and guidelines for surveillance of
     country exchange rate systems are specified in a series of board
     decisions, first adopted in 1977 and revised in later years. These are
     published in the IMF's *Selected Decisions and Selected Documents*,
     cited above, pp.10-29. Reference here is to the General Principles,
     Principles for the Guidance of Members' Exchange Rate Policies, and
     Principles of Fund Surveillance over Exchange Rate Policies specified

in the IMF board decision *Surveillance over Exchange Rate Policies: Review,* Decision No. 6026-(9/13), January 22, 1979, as amended, pp. 10-16.

[6]   Morris Goldstein argues that efforts to maintain a country's exchange rate at a fixed level over a long period of time, despite changes in domestic and international economic conditions, are just as much evidence of manipulation as are efforts to change a currency's international advantage in order to achieve short term trade advantage. See his "China and the Renminbi Exchange Rate." in C. Fred Bergsten and John Williamson, ed. *Dollar Adjustment: How Far? Against Whom?* Washington, D.C.: Institute for International Economics, November 2004. Special Report 17.

[7]   The Central Bank of China is located in Taiwan and serves the Republic of China. The term "central bank" in this paper will refer to the People's Bank of China.

[8]   The new procedure was widely discussed in the press. See, for example, "2% Solution: China lets Yuan Rise vs. Dollar, Easing Trade Tensions Slightly." *Wall Street Journal*, July 22, 2005, p. 1; Richard McGregor *et al.* "China revalues the renminbi." *Financial Times*, July 22, 2005, p. 1; and Peter Goodman. "China Ends Fixed-Rate Currency." *Washington Post*, July 22, 2005, p. 1.

[9]   See, for example, Mure Dickie and Andrew Balls. "Beijing cools currency hopes." *Financial Times,* July 27, 2005, p. 1. See also Peter Goodman. "Don't Expect Yuan to Rise Much, China Tells World." *Washington Post*, July 27, 2005, p. D1.

[10]   *Financial Times. Ibid.*

[11]   See, for example: Morris Goldstein and Nicholas Lardy. "China's revaluation shows size really matters." *Financial Times,* July 22, 2005, p. 13.

[12]   Beijing cools currency hopes. Note 9.

[13]   Ibid.

[14]   Anjali Athavaley. "Schumer, Graham May Press for China Tariffs." *Washington Post*, July 29, 2005, p. D5.

[15]   International Monetary Fund. *Annual Report on Exchange Arrangements and Exchange Restrictions, 2004.* Washington, D.C., 2004, p. 218.

[16]   *Op. Cit.*, note 3.

[17]   [U.S. Department of the Treasury.] *Report to Congress on International Economic and Exchange Rate Policies, May 2005.*

Obtained from [http://www.treas/gov], the Treasury Department website. See especially pp. 11-14.

[18] See, for example Andrew Balls, "US sets out revaluation deadline for China," *Financial Times*, USA edition, May 18, 2005, p. 1. See also Edmund L. Andrews, "Bush's Choice: Anger China or Congress over Currency," *The New York Times*, May 17, 2005, p. 1, Donna Borak, "U.S. increases pressure on China's currency," *UPI Perspectives*, May 24, 2005, and Andrew Balls, "FT.com site: China told to revalue by 10% by US," *Financial Times*, May 24, 2005, p. 1.

[19] Snow Welcomes China's Currency Reforms, at [http://www.treas.gov/news/index1.html].

[20] Susie Gharib. "Secretary of State John Snow Sounds-off On China's Money Move." *Nightly Business Review*, July 21, 2005. Interview, available at [http://www.nightltybusiness.org/transcript.html].

[21] Greg Hitt. "Senate Slams China's Currency Policy." *Wall Street Journal.* April 7, 2005, 1. For a list of all current congressional legislation aimed at the Chinese exchange rate issue, see. *U.S.-China Trade Issues*, note 1.

[22] *Ibid.*

[23] "China revalues, cited earlier, from *Financial Times*, July 21, 2005, p. 1.

[24] Nancy E. Kelly. "China's currency policies prompt 'cheat' accusations House bill would ease trade complaint filings." *American Metal Market*, April 8, 2005, V iii, I 13-15, P 1(2).

[25] See, for example: "Richard McGregor. "Aim is to allow greater flexibility while still keeping firm control." and "Making sense of China's choice." *Financial Times*, July 22, 2005, pp. 2 and 4.

[26] Paul Brent. "Dodge's call to free the Chinese yuan has strong backing." *National Post* (Don Mills, Ontario), June 6, 2005, p. FP2.

[27] "Tanigaki says quick action on yuan needed." *Economic Times of India., The Electronic Times* Online, July 9, 2005. See the *Economic Times of India*'s website at [http://economictimes.indiatimes.com/articleshow/1165902.cms].   By contrast, Japan previously had called for China to take immediate action. The Japanese Finance Minister told the G7 finance ministers in February 2003 meeting, that change was urgently needed and "Too much importation of China's cheap goods" was "the root-cause of the global economic depression." Yang Jian and Melinda Moore. "Renminbi" Eurobiz Magazine, July 2003, found at [http://www.sinomedia.net/eurobiz/v200307/rmb.html].

[28] Kervin Yao and Yoko Nishikawa. "Yuan Dominates Asia-Europe meeting." *Reuters*, June 26, 2005, reported at [http://news.yahoo.com/s/nm/economy_china_dc&printer].

[29] Cary Huang. "World clamours for Beijing to revalue yuan; But there is agreement that China should dictate timing of any currency reforms." *South China Post* (Hong Kong), June 27, 2005, p. 5. The EU finance minister said that China should do what it thought best. Cindi Sui. "Europe backs off on yuan value." *The Australian*, June 27, 2005, at [http://theaustralian.news.com.au/common/story_page/0,5744,157417 09%255E31037,00 .htm].

[30] Scott Hills. "China's Hu sidesteps yuan debate in G8 address." *Reuters*, July 1, 2005, at [http://today.reuters/PrinterFriendlyPopup.aspx?type=live8News&Stor yiD-uri:2005-o.html].

[31] "G8 summit offers Hu a window to adjust yuan policy." *South China Morning Post* (Hong Kong), July 6, 2005, p. 2.

[32] International Monetary Fund. *People's Republic of China: Staff Report for the 2004 Article IV Consultation.* July 6, 2004, p. 12. This report is available from the IMF website at [http://www.imf.org/external/pubs/ft/scr/2004/cr04351.pdf].

[33] *Ibid*, pp. 11-13. The staff report stressed that greater exchange rate flexibility would "enhance China's ability to purse an independent monetary policy and adjust to shocks." The staff also found that tighter monetary policy would help China slow its rate of growth to a more sustainable pace, that money and credit growth needed to be reduced but that large capital inflows (from investment and trade) were making it increasingly difficult for Chinese authorities to control money and credit growth. The staff reported that the authorities were worried that a large change in the value of the yuan would increase unemployment. The IMF staff said, however, that balanced and sustainable growth would "provide the best conditions to stimulate employment growth" and that "increased flexibility of the exchange rate would improve the effectiveness of monetary policy in reducing overheating risks." The staff also asserted that, despite China's assertions to the contrary, that increased exchange rate flexibility would not pose substantial risks for the banking system given the limited scale of the system's foreign assets and liabilities.

[34] International Monetary Fund. *IMF Concludes 2004 Article IV Consultation with the People's Republic of China*, August 25, 2004

Public Information Notice 04/99. It appears from context that "greater flexibility" meant an upward valuation of the yuan.

[35] "US Treasury Welcomes," *Financial Times*, July 22, 2005, note 20.

[36] For the IMF executive board to have issued a statement of this sort, most major countries would have had to vote for it and some would have had a hand in its preparation.

[37] The IMF's guidelines for surveillance over exchange rate policies say that, "taking into account any views that have been expressed by other members," the Managing Director may consider whether a country's policies are in accord with the Fund's exchange rate principles and undertake informal and confidential discussions with the country on that issue. Depending on his findings, the Managing Director is required to report his or her findings formally or informally to the executive board. In the past, Germany has filed such a complaint about Sweden and the United States has filed a complaint about Korea. IMF surveillance guidelines, note 8.

[38] See Arrangement for Consultation and Cooperation with the Contracting Parties of GATT, September 9, 1948, and Guidelines/Framework for Fund Staff Collaboration with the World Trade Organization, April 21, 1995. Both are included in the IMF's Selected Decisions and Selected Documents of the International Monetary Fund, pp. 546-9 and 552-9 of the 24th issue. Washington, D.C. June 30, 1999.

INDEX

D

Q

R

S

White House, 47
words, 38, 48, 62, 76
work, 26, 65, 71, 72, 75, 76, 78
workers, 1, 4, 9, 11, 12, 30, 33, 36, 51, 52, 55
World Bank, 45
World Trade Organization, 37, 54, 58, 69, 71, 73, 77, 82
worry, 53, 60, 64
WTO, 30, 37, 40, 41, 42, 43, 44, 50, 54, 58, 69, 71, 73, 77, 78

Y

yuan, vii, 1, 2, 3, 4, 5, 6, 8, 11, 12, 15, 17, 19, 20, 21, 22, 23, 24, 25, 26, 30, 31, 32, 35, 37, 38, 39, 45, 47, 48, 53, 55, 57, 58, 59, 60, 63, 64, 65, 66, 68, 70, 71, 72, 73, 75, 77, 78, 80, 81, 82